IMAGES
of America

LOMA LINDA

MOUND CITY STORE

BY THE RAILROAD TRACKS

Two Phones: Loma Linda, 222
Redlands, Green 1635

GROCERIES—At Money-Saving Low Prices.

Specials for Thurs. and Fri.

Milk, tall cans, 3 for .... .25
Oleomargarine, 2 pounds .... .33
Wright's Mayonnaise, extra quality, pint jar .... .45
Heinz oven baked beans, large cans, 2 for .... .25
Peas, three seive, early june, No. 2 cans, 2 for .... .25
Corn, Iowa sugar, No. 2 can, 2 for .... .21
Orange honey, quart jar .... .55
Walnuts, Placentia budded, 5 pounds 1.00
Crisco, 6 pound pail 1.45
White King washing powder, large pkg. .... .39
Lux toilet soap, 4 bars .... .27
Kansas cleanser, 4 cans .... .33
Bananas, 4 pounds .... .25
Muscat grapes, 4 pounds .... .25
Seedless grapes, 6 pounds .... .25
Bartlet pears, 4 pounds .... .25
Fontana macaroni, 4 pkgs. .... .25
Premium soda crackers, 3 pound box .... .43
Cookies, assorted 2 pounds .... .35

Summer underware for men, B.V.D. or Gotham **75c**
knit, 1.50 value, per suit ....

This advertisement appeared in *The Argus* on September 19, 1929.

ON THE COVER: The W. F. Whittier citrus packing shed in Bryn Mawr, pictured around 1900, was one of four locally owned packinghouses that sped the community's "golden harvest" to eastern markets via the Southern Pacific Railroad.

IMAGES
of America

LOMA LINDA

Loma Linda Historical Commission

ARCADIA
PUBLISHING

Published by Arcadia Publishing
Charleston SC, Chicago IL, Portsmouth NH, San Francisco CA

Library of Congress Catalog Card Number: 2005932500

For all general information contact Arcadia Publishing at:
Telephone 843-853-2070
Fax 843-853-0044
E-mail sales@arcadiapublishing.com
For customer service and orders:
Toll-Free 1-888-313-2665

Visit us on the Internet at www.arcadiapublishing.com

Bryn Mawr oranges were known nationwide as some of the sweetest.

CONTENTS

ACKNOWLEDGMENTS

This project would not have been possible without the help and support of the following groups and individuals: archivist Petre Cimpoeru and director Marilyn Crane of the Heritage Room at the Del E. Webb Memorial Library at Loma Linda University for research assistance and use of numerous images from their vast collection; Nathan Gonzales and the A. K. Smiley Library Heritage Room for the use of their images; Michele Nielsen and the San Bernardino County Museum for assistance with dating photographs and the use of museum images; architectural historian Roger Hathaway for invaluable assistance in locating long-forgotten images and reports as well as a first-rate introduction; Michael Stewart, Joe Frink, Hale Paxton, Dick Wiley, and Nellie Rodriguez for sharing family photographs of earlier times in old Bryn Mawr and Mission Road; Jackie Moncrieff, Elmer Digneo, Betty Stark, and Kenneth and Virginia Wical for allowing their family photographs of the Loma Linda community to be published; Fire Marshal Rolland M. Crawford for graciously opening the archives of the Loma Linda Fire Department to us; and Deborah Woldruff, director of community development for the City of Loma Linda, for support and encouragement. Most importantly, we would like to thank the people who keep our community's history alive in the public discourse, the Loma Linda Historical Commission: vice chairman Michael Stewart, William B. Coffman, Elmer J. Digneo, Georgia E. Hodgkin, Fred Ramos, Marilyn Crane, Betty Stark, Rudy Szutz, and Dick Wiley.

—Jim Shipp, Chairman
Loma Linda Historical Commission

INTRODUCTION

This book contains treasure. It documents the growth and development of a truly remarkable community utilizing the miracle of the historic photograph. The fact that many of these images survive is a miracle in and of itself, but the manner in which the Loma Linda Historical Commission, chaired by author, educator, and preservationist Jim Shipp, has assembled these photographs brings time and times past miraculously alive by spotlighting those many historic jewels that are a part of the history of Loma Linda. The city named after a "beautiful hill" has a beauty truly all its own.

Loma Linda is my favorite small city in southern California. I first encountered this wonderful place in 1987 when, at the request of a now retired but environmentally friendly and far-sighted city planner, I was asked to prepare a proposal to conduct an architectural and historical survey of the entire city. This was nothing new to me, as my job for the last 30 years has involved the preparation of historical, architectural, and archaeological surveys for everything ranging from a single property, to a proposed new housing tract, to a military base, to an entire city. What was new to me was the incredible variety of "treasure" I found in the cultural resources I inventoried in Loma Linda.

The survey submitted to the City of Loma Linda recorded a stunning variety of cultural resource types. It included California Mission sites, historic adobes, the almost unknown town of Old San Bernardino, 19th-century or American Period farmhouses, residential mansions and villas, the birthplace of the citrus industry in San Bernardino County, the remains of a 19th-century resort and sanitarium, a railroad siding turned community center, ethnic landmarks, the birthplace of one of the most successful and best known Seventh-day Adventist communities in the world, a historic hospital and university buildings, and several architectural and historical districts. I had never seen such an amazing range and depth of cultural resources in such a small geographic area in southern California. I was astounded then and still am today.

Historically, Loma Linda presents itself as a series of communities that would appear, at first glance, to be entirely dissimilar. However, when viewed through the long lens of history they become remarkably alike. These communities include the Native American/Mission period (prior to the early 1830s), the Rancho to American periods (ranching, settlement and farming prior to 1900), and the early-20th-century Seventh-day Adventist enclave. Quite simply, the lands of Loma Linda appear to have fostered, extending across time, a powerful and pervasive sense of community that is as unique as the range of resource landmarks themselves.

This sense of community was first expressed in the region later known as Loma Linda from prehistoric times to the Mission period. Native Americans are known to have established a large village near the mouth of San Timoteo Canyon, and this group was ultimately incorporated into the San Gabriel Mission system. Completed around 1820, Native Americans built, under the direction of San Gabriel Mission representatives, the Mill Creek Zanja, one of the most important engineering achievements in the entire Inland Empire in the first half of the 19th century.

The second community to develop in Loma Linda was centered in the Mission District, or what was later known as Old San Bernardino. Beginning in the 1850s, this was the first permanent American-period settlement established in San Bernardino County. It developed as an agricultural community, with extremely close family ties and a high degree of dependence on one's neighbor. This community would include a railroad siding, a small town center, fruit-packing houses, and the Mission District school system. Today the Mission District and the Zanja are recognized by local preservation ordinances.

The third community to develop in Loma Linda begins in 1905 with the establishment of the Seventh-day Adventist enclave. This initiates the modern development of the city and begins an odyssey that can only be described as unique to southern California. From humble beginnings, the Seventh-day Adventist community has grown to include a world-class hospital and university. The lifestyle that is a part of the Seventh-day Adventist faith has itself created an amazingly coherent community. Throughout most of the 20th century, doctors, dentists, reverends, medical superintendents, elders, and educators are found living next door to nurses, laundry workers, plumbers, carpenters, and students. Today Loma Linda is, in fact, a wonderful melting pot of humankind, held together and made whole by strong Seventh-day Adventist bonds.

The people of Loma Linda are, of course, at the center of all that is magic in this city. From prehistoric times to the present, the people of Loma Linda have been nurtured by and created wonderful things on the land within eyesight of the original beautiful hill. This book records the amazing historical odyssey that is Loma Linda. The care with which it has been assembled demonstrates that the author is both a part of and has been deeply moved by the very sense of community that has made Loma Linda a very special place from time immemorial.

—Roger Hatheway
Architectural Historian

One

BEFORE THE
AMERICAN FLOOD

Fredrico Terrones, photographed by Mission School students for a history project in 1917, was one of only two living Mission Indians still in the Loma Linda area. Known as "Chico," he worked on the George M. Cooley ranch. (Courtesy San Bernardino County Archives.)

Maxine Strane published *Tomo of Kukumonga Village* in 1975 to show elementary school students how the hunter-gatherers of the valley lived before European influence. This illustration from the book, drawn by her husband, Ralph Strane, shows the natives of Kukumonga Village rebuilding their homes after a fierce Santa Ana wind. The book is available at the Rains House in Rancho Cucamonga. (Courtesy Maxine and Ralph Strane.)

Games and festivities were held in this open field by Native Americans of the Loma Linda area. The exact location is known only by a reference to being at the foot of the hill by "Alec Fowler's place" in the Mission School history report of 1917. (Courtesy San Bernardino County Archives.)

When Spanish missionaries arrived in the San Bernardino Valley in 1819 to establish an outpost of the San Gabriel Mission, they realized they needed a reliable water supply. With natives supplying the work force, this *zanja* ("ditch" in Spanish) was dug from Mill Creek to the mission farm near the west end of Mission Road. The *zanja*, seen here in 1917 in the Mission District, provided water to farmers who lived beside it for over 100 years, although water rights became hotly contested. (Courtesy San Bernardino County Archives.)

There are no known photographs of the adobe building that served as a storehouse and granary for the Spanish mission *estancia* (farm) on Mission Road. It was only a few years before the missionaries realized they had chosen a location in the flood zone of San Timoteo Creek. A new mission outpost was built in 1831 at the location of the Asistencia in Redlands. This drawing of unknown origin is based on descriptions of the 1820 mission building by Mission Road. (Courtesy San Bernardino County Museum.)

Don Antonio Maria Lugo was already a successful cattle rancher when he acquired the San Bernardino Valley from the Mexican government for a token payment of $800, which was to be paid in cattle hides. (Courtesy A. K. Smiley Library.)

With the San Bernardino Mountains as its northern and eastern borders, Slover Mountain to the west, and the hills of Loma Linda as its southern boundary, the Lugo ranch encompassed over 35,000 acres. Lugo's sons, Jose Maria, Jose del Carmen, and Vicente and close family friend Jose Diego Sepulveda settled around the valley and raised cattle.

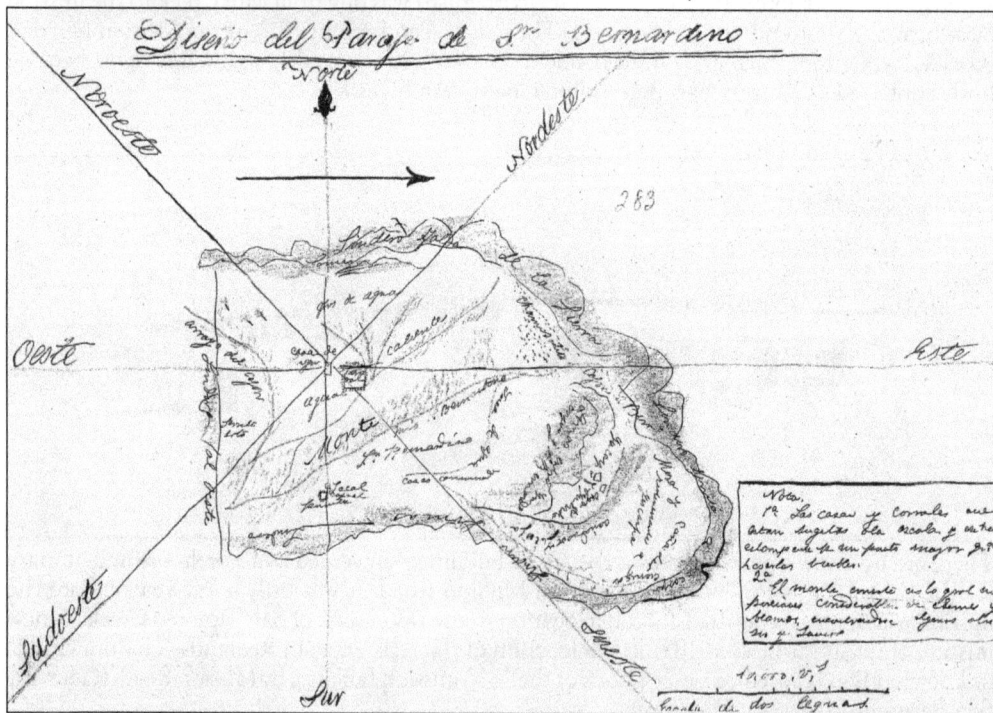

Two

FIRST RESORT

Who could resist? The first attempts at settling Loma Linda were financial failures. By 1888, substantial money was being invested to build a first-rate resort near the all-important Southern Pacific railway tracks. Even this idyllic artist's rendering couldn't woo enough potential visitors to keep the grand hotel profitable. (Courtesy A. K. Smiley Library.)

LOMA LINDA

The Switzerland of America

In the foothills of the San Bernardino Mountains, on the main line of the Southern Pacific Railroad. ❧ ❧

Where Health and Pleasure are Twins

An Elegant Health Hotel

Is this Switzerland? It was a real stretch to describe the inland desert as alpine. Perhaps the gullible reader of this 1900 pamphlet might be beguiled, but one look at the reality of Loma Linda's location kept him on the train. Rules for the 1900 transition from resort hotel to sanitarium kept out consumptives (people with tuberculosis) or anyone else extremely sick. (Courtesy A. K. Smiley Library.)

There was no question that the structure and grounds were beautiful. The builders spent over $40,000 constructing the Mound City Villa, which eventually evolved into the Loma Linda Sanitarium. (Courtesy Del E. Webb Library, Loma Linda University.)

In a day when horses provided most transportation, the arrival of the railroad was a cause for celebration. The train changed the trip from Los Angeles to Loma Linda from a weeklong ordeal to a comfortable ride of an hour or so. Loma Linda's train station languished until the arrival of the Seventh-day Adventists in 1905. (Courtesy Del E. Webb Library, Loma Linda University.)

15

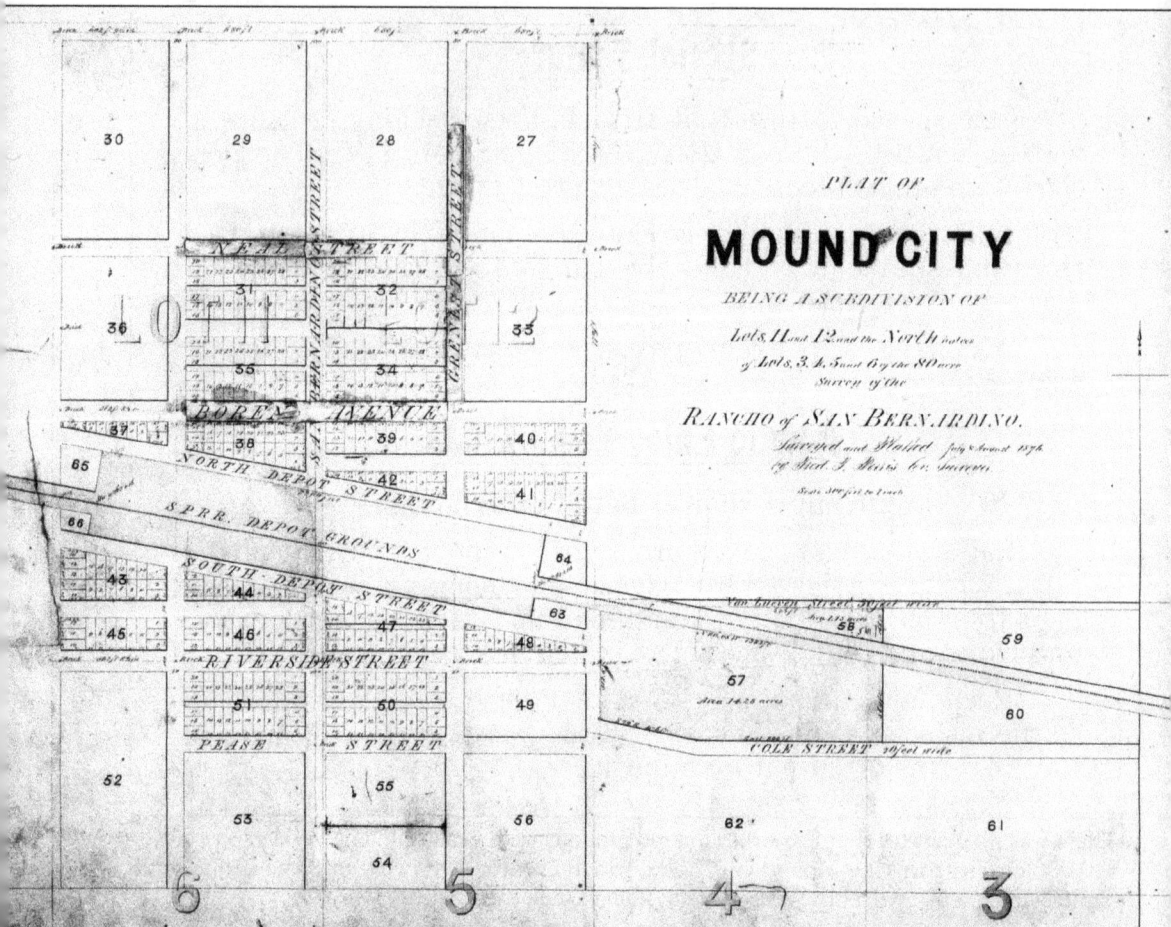

As soon as surveys for the Southern Pacific Railroad were finalized, developers proposed town sites all along the route. This map of Mound City, surveyed by legendary pioneer Fred Perris in 1876, was the first of three failures to capitalize on Loma Linda's location by the rails. (Courtesy San Bernardino County Archives.)

Changing the name to Loma Linda ("pretty hill" in Spanish) in 1900 was accompanied by writing the name on the northern slope of the Mound. Some say the lettering was made of whitewashed hay bales. Somehow the potential visitors still managed to stay on the train. (Courtesy Del E. Webb Library, Loma Linda University.)

The railroad was the key for paying customers to stop in Loma Linda. Getting them from the station to the sanitarium involved a strenuous climb or a buggy ride that circled up the Mound. (Courtesy Del E. Webb Library, Loma Linda University.)

17

When retired sea captain Lewis Smith Davis was looking for a place to settle in 1895, he landed in Mound City. His house and the palms he had just planted along Prospect Avenue are still around today. His expansive groves have been replaced by homes and apartments. (Courtesy Del E. Webb Library, Loma Linda University.)

It's said that only the railroad station sign survived the 1916 flood. Someone pulled it off the building, saying "I'm not going to have Loma Linda floating downstream!" (Courtesy Del E. Webb Library, Loma Linda University.)

18

Three

WORLDS APART

The Frink brothers, Alonzo and Marcus, opened this establishment in 1916. They had built an earlier store in 1896, which was operated in turn by Nathan Stone, Carl Smith, Billie Ruce, and Leonard Bahr. Bahr later turned the old store into a pool hall and restaurant, building a larger store beside it. (Courtesy Joe Frink.)

Anson Van Leuven was 25 years old when his Mormon family arrived in the San Bernardino Valley in 1854. He helped build the first Mission School beside the *zanja* and went on to be sheriff, deputy U.S. marshal, state representative, and citrus pioneer. His home still stands at 10664 Mountain View Avenue in Loma Linda. (Courtesy Hale Paxton.)

This is a true covered-wagon pioneer. Frederick Van Leuven, along with his 10 children, brother Benjamin and his 8 children, and all their earthly goods, arrived in Loma Linda in 1854. Although Latter-day Saints, they chose to remain in the Mission Road area when a majority of Mormons returned to Utah in 1857. (Courtesy Hale Paxton.)

No one exemplifies the Americanization of California more than Horace Monroe Frink. Born in 1831, Frink was a childhood friend of Brigham Young, second Prophet and leader of the Latter-day Saints. Fifteen-year-old Horace drove a wagon for Young across the country in the Mormon Exodus of 1847, then set off to seek his fortune in the West. (Courtesy Joe Frink.)

What mother would want to see her teenage son take off for the Wild West? Sybil Lathrop, mother of Horace Monroe Frink, apparently followed the family, as evidenced by this glass-plate image. (Courtesy Joe Frink.)

John Harris, Lewis F. Cram, and the Cram brothers built a water-powered woodworking shop to harness the power of the *zanja* in 1854. They built furniture, including these chairs, for three years. Their furniture was widely regarded as the first manufactured furniture in Southern California. (Courtesy San Bernardino County Archives.)

The Van Leuven family reunions were legendary at the turn of the century, often numbering a 100 or more members. The Van Leuvens, Frinks, and other Mission Road pioneer families sometimes married and the resulting clan had a significant impact on the local economy and government. This reunion, around 1890, numbers about 70 family members. (Courtesy Joe Frink.)

Marcus Frink, second from left, and other unidentified gun-toting pioneers demonstrate the firepower necessary to safeguard the gold shipments that the Frink family hauled in the 1800s. (Courtesy Joe Frink.)

The Redlands & San Bernardino Railroad connected the two cities, passing along Mission Road. Nicknamed "the Dinky," it enjoyed a short but popular run connecting the south end of the valley. (Courtesy A. K. Smiley Library.)

The second generation to live in the Frink adobe included Lorana Van Leuven Frink, Alonzo M. Frink, and daughter Patience Frink, pictured here in a studio portrait. (Courtesy Hale Paxton.)

Idlewild was a short-lived town site at the present corner of Mountain View Avenue and Redlands Boulevard. Like other stores of the area, proprietors changed quickly. Dr. Pearson built the first store in 1888, which burned in 1898 after being run in succession by J. H. Bear, I. M. Broadwell, John Lawrence, M. Simmons, and A. McCrary. A second store was built in 1901 for A. G. Kelley, which burned in 1903. (Courtesy San Bernardino County Museum.)

Redlands became famous overnight after its founding by Edward Judson and Frank Brown in 1881. Rivalry between the Santa Fe, which served Redlands, and the Southern Pacific, which passed through Mound City, meant that Southern Pacific passengers traveling to Redlands needed a station nearby. Passengers alighting at Redlands Junction (later Bryn Mawr) could take a narrow-gauge railcar to Redlands or San Bernardino. (Courtesy San Bernardino County Museum.)

Lizzie Frink married L. R. Bahr in 1902. He took over the Frink Brothers store, adding a larger and more elaborate building, pictured here, on Main Street in Bryn Mawr. (Courtesy Hale Paxton.)

Bahr's store was eventually converted into this service station. Note the gravity-feed gasoline pumps out front and the ominous warning, "Please do not park in front of pumps." (Courtesy Hale Paxton.)

This home near the Bryn Mawr railroad depot, although small and simple by current standards, had electricity. Building off the ground helped when the San Timoteo Creek flooded. See Chapter 7 for more about floods. (Courtesy Hale Paxton.)

DREW AND CRAWFORD'S SUBDIVISON
OF THE
BRYN-MAWR-TRACT
ADJOINING MOUND-CITY. SAN BERNARDINO CO.
1888

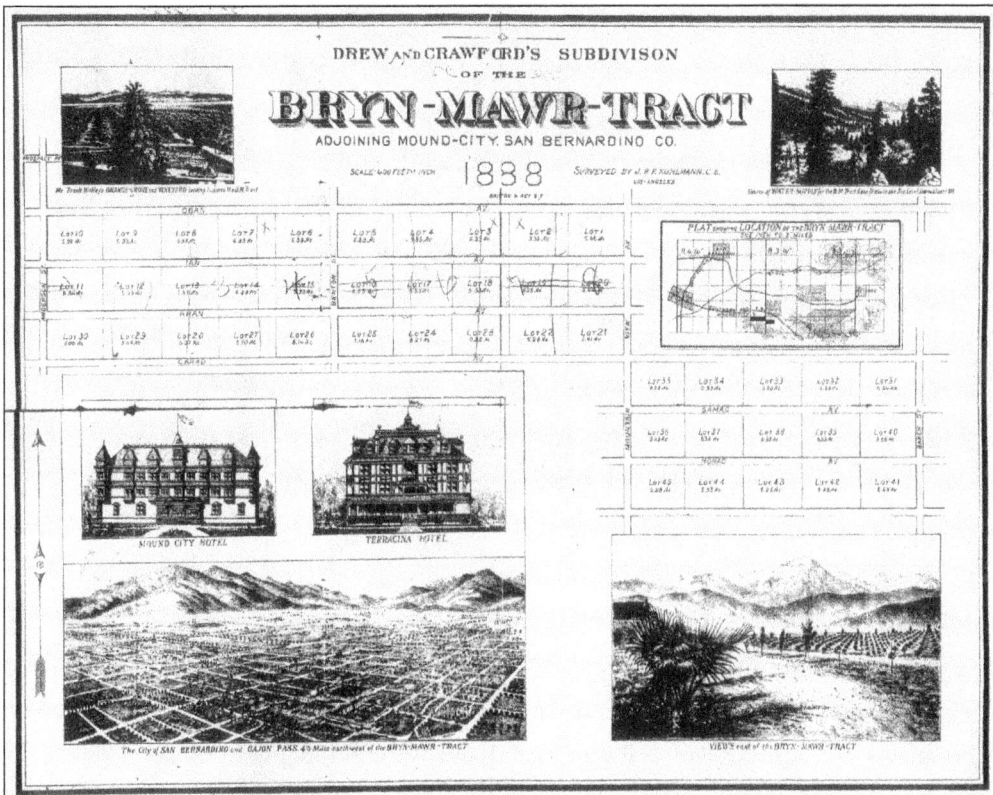

H. L. Drew was an enterprising banker and citrus rancher. He envisioned a vast community built on his land, to be called "Bryn Mawr." A recession dampened the success of the venture. Only one house remains of the 1888 development, at the corner of Mount View and Carad Street, now Lawton Avenue. (Courtesy City of Loma Linda.)

Railroad travel was still the best way to get to Los Angeles and other faraway places. World War II created shortages in fuel and supplies, so the Pacific Electric Company advertised in the Loma Linda Directory in 1945, thanking patrons for their patience during "these trying times."

Thanks for Your Help

We thank you, the traveling public, for the kind co-operation you have shown during these trying times. We appreciate the many seemingly unimportant things like making room for that extra person, moving to the rear of the coaches, having correct fare ready, and avoiding rush hours when possible for necessary trips.

We will continue to do our utmost to provide reliable and convenient transportation service.

KEEP ON BUYING WAR BONDS

PACIFIC ELECTRIC
RAIL AND MOTOR COACH *Lines*

The Nelson family, pictured here in 1909, built a home above what is now Hulda Crooks Park. (Courtesy Betty Stark and Carol Nelson.)

This was the only home on Hinckley Avenue. Historical Commissioner Dick Wiley lived in the house until it was demolished in 1979 to make way for new housing. (Courtesy Dick Wiley.)

Four

HEALTHY DECISIONS

John Burden bought Loma Linda Sanitarium in 1905 at the urging of Seventh-day Adventist pioneer Ellen G. White. He used $1,000 of his own money as down payment for the $40,000 price. The sanitarium had a stock value of $300,000 in 1901 but had not been profitable for the owners. (Courtesy Del E. Webb Library, Loma Linda University.)

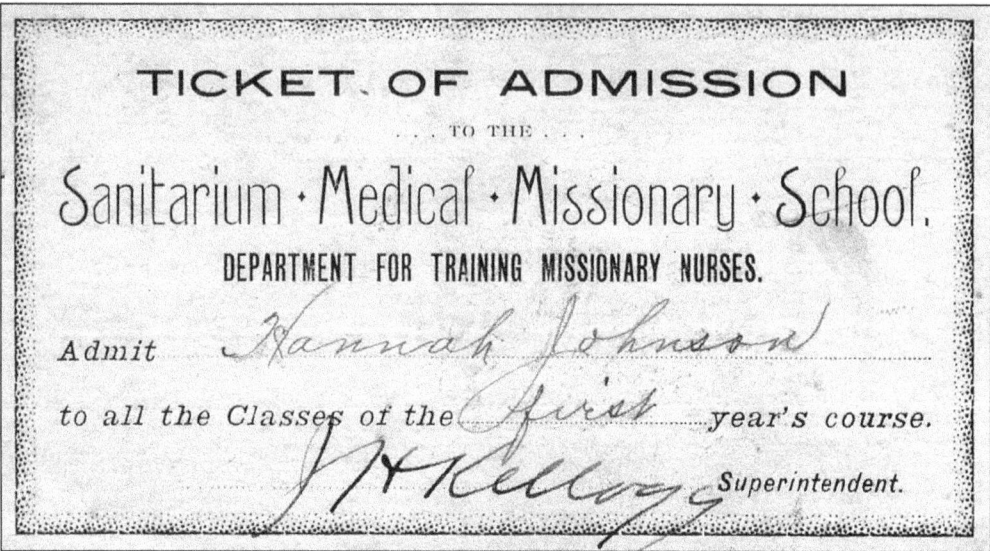

TICKET OF ADMISSION

... TO THE ...

Sanitarium · Medical · Missionary · School.

DEPARTMENT FOR TRAINING MISSIONARY NURSES.

Admit *Hannah Johnson*

to all the Classes of the *first* year's course.

J H Kellogg, Superintendent.

Loma Linda was a continuation of the Seventh-day Adventist medical program begun at Battle Creek, Michigan. John Harvey Kellogg signed Hannah Johnson's admission to the nursing school at Battle Creek. Hannah, mother of Elmer Digneo, relocated to Loma Linda to join the new sanitarium. (Courtesy Elmer Digneo.)

A sanitarium needed highly trained nurses to carry out the innovative treatments prescribed for the sick people who arrived by train and buggy. The first class, pictured here, was small, but the school of nursing grew quickly. (Courtesy Del E. Webb Library, Loma Linda University.)

30

The Seventh-day Adventist treatment program included strict dietary guidelines, including vegetarianism, exercise, fresh air, sunshine, and plenty of water inside and out. Hydrotherapy was good for circulation and the mind. (Courtesy Del E. Webb Library, Loma Linda University.)

Hydrotherapy treatments became more and more sophisticated as equipment was developed to treat the body with hot and cold water. (Courtesy Del E. Webb Library, Loma Linda University.)

31

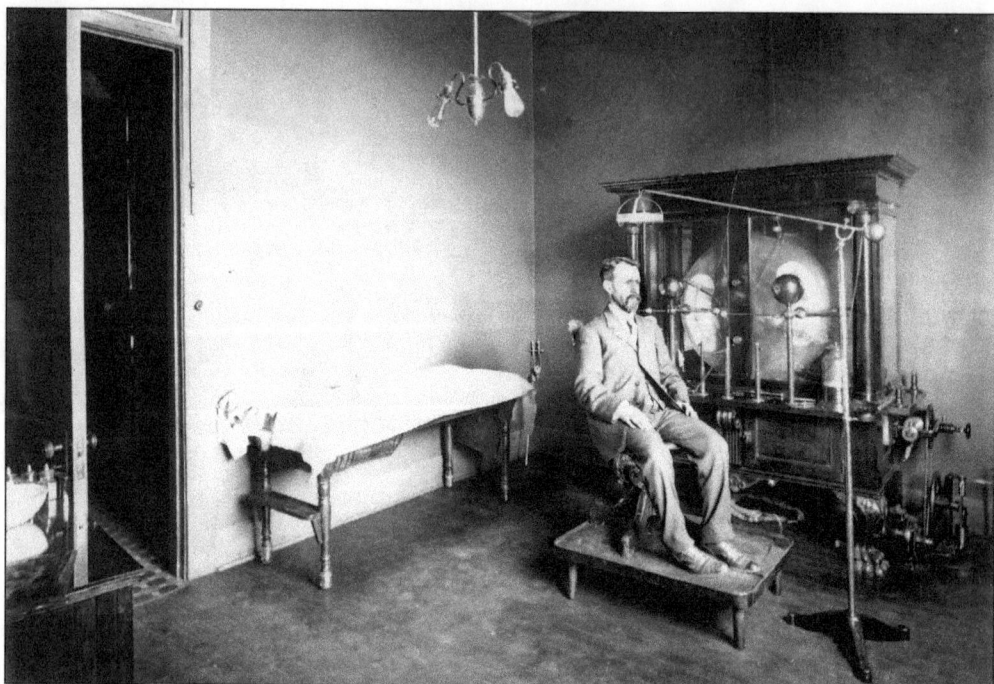

Milton Eskey, manager of the sanitarium before the Seventh-day Adventist takeover, purchased expensive static-electricity-treatment equipment. It was thought that electrical treatments stimulated the mind and body and aided healing. (Courtesy A. K. Smiley Library.)

Where can you get a good vegetarian meal around here? In the early 1900s, markets catered to meat-eating people. Factories in Battle Creek and Loma Linda became famous worldwide for dried and canned foods that supplied vegetable protein for vegetarians. (Courtesy Del E. Webb Library, Loma Linda University.)

When Loma Linda expanded its program to include a medical school, there was a scramble to provide a solid scientific education for its graduates. These medical students are studying in a well-stocked chemistry classroom. (Courtesy A. K. Smiley Library.)

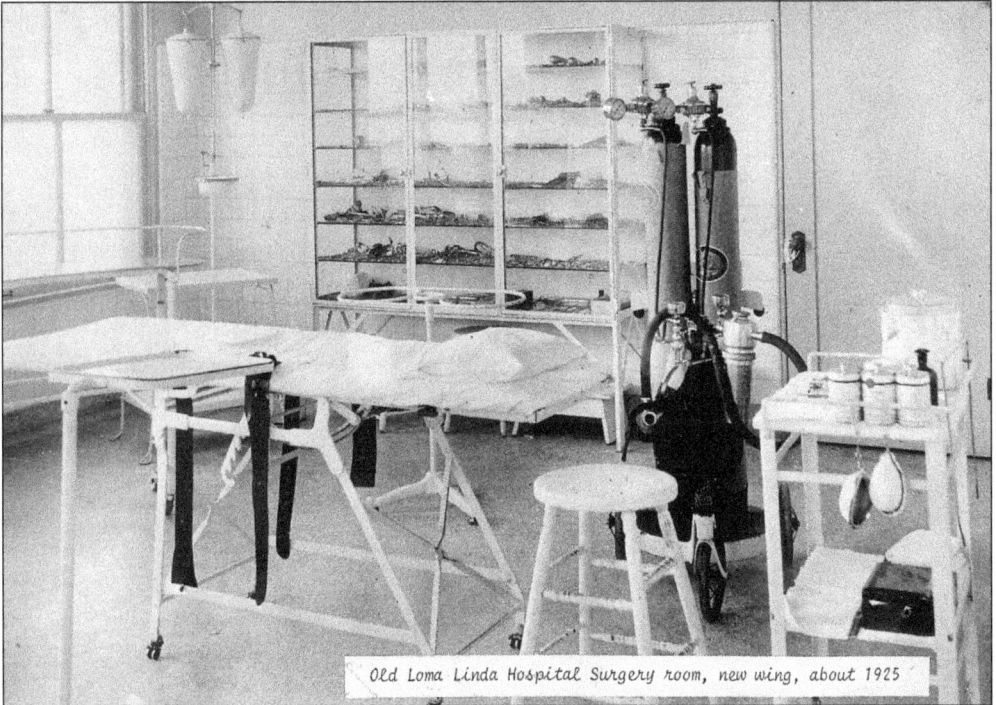

Old Loma Linda Hospital Surgery room, new wing, about 1925

Antiseptic surgery was relatively new, and this 1925 surgical room, although Spartan by our standards, was clean and well-equipped for its time. (Courtesy Del E. Webb Library, Loma Linda University.)

The Loma Linda Sanitarium came equipped with equestrian facilities and exercise areas, including this covered croquet court, for quiet, relaxing play. (Courtesy Del E. Webb Library, Loma Linda University.)

Many people were suffering from illnesses caused by polluted city water and air. Tending the sanitarium garden brought patients back in contact with healthy exercise in the fresh air and sunshine. (Courtesy Del E. Webb Library, Loma Linda University.)

Exercise was expected of everyone recovering at Loma Linda Sanitarium from the stresses of modern life. These patients are exercising on the croquet court. (Courtesy Del E. Webb Library, Loma Linda University.)

The sanitarium expanded with a true hospital in 1913, built on the west end of the campus. It was quickly replaced with a new sanitarium on the top of the Mound in 1929. (Courtesy Del E. Webb Library, Loma Linda University.)

THRU THE PALMS —
Loma Linda Sanitarium, Loma Linda, Calif.

It took huge quantities of water to turn the sanitarium grounds into lush gardens. Artesian wells and pumps kept the village and institutions well supplied. (Courtesy Del E. Webb Library, Loma Linda University.)

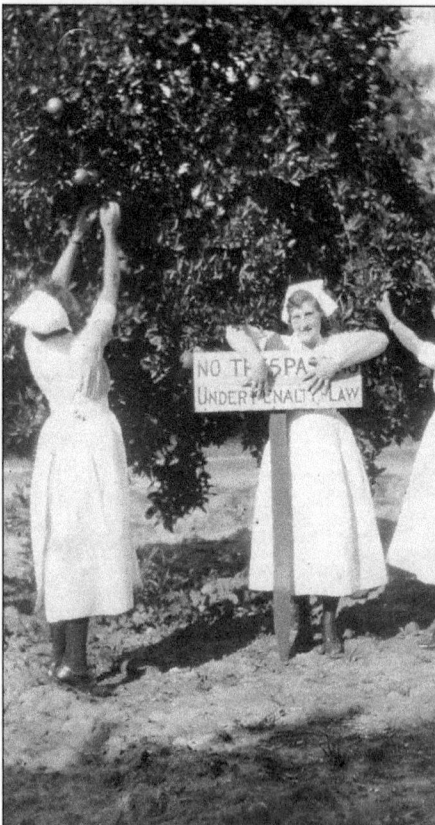

There were orange groves surrounding the Mound at one time. Patients were regularly treated to this healthy fruit, so rare and expensive in other parts of the country. (Courtesy Del E. Webb Library, Loma Linda University.)

Dr. Daniel Hartman Kress plucks the "orange gold" from the sanitarium's grove. (Courtesy Del E. Webb Library, Loma Linda University.)

Health food was a vital export for people extolling the virtue of living without eating meat. (Courtesy Del E. Webb Library, Loma Linda University.)

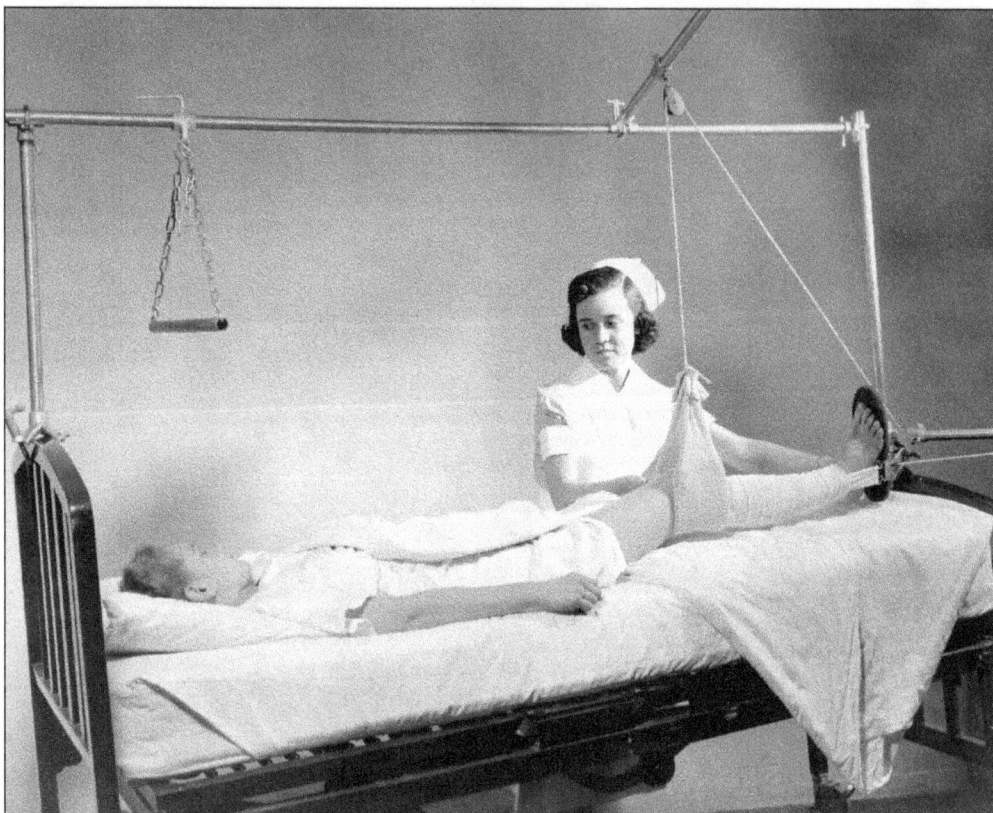

Nurses in the class of 1943 were taught the latest techniques in medical care. Student Zella Morrow demonstrates traction techniques while Jackie Unger acts as patient. (Courtesy Jackie Moncreiff.)

Graduating from the College of Medical Evangelists in 1943, nurse Jackie Unger sports the scarlet cape that was a symbol of achievement and the white cap that identified graduate nurses for so long. (Courtesy Jackie Moncrieff.)

These 35 members of the nursing school class of 1943 gather for this photograph at graduation. The school had certainly grown since 1906. (Courtesy Jackie Moncrieff.)

As the population of the valley grew, so did the demand on the sanitarium. This new facility, at the top of the Mound, cost over $1 million to build in 1929, just at the start of the Great Depression. (Courtesy Del E. Webb Library, Loma Linda University.)

Loma Linda had its own bowl in the first half of the 20th century on the north side of the Mound. The noise of train bells and whistles caused regular disruption of graduations and other ceremonies. (Courtesy Del E. Webb Library, Loma Linda University.)

Although electric power came early to the area, sanitarium leaders recognized that a hospital needed its own reliable power supply. This "old" power plant near the railroad tracks was replaced later by a cogeneration plant near the dental school that provides power, steam, cooling water, and many other services for the entire university system. (Courtesy Del E. Webb Library, Loma Linda University.)

In 1913, these students and teachers are off in a sanitarium truck equipped as an open-air bus to conduct health classes in the community. (Courtesy Del E. Webb Library, Loma Linda University.)

Perhaps nothing influenced the economy, size, and reputation of Loma Linda as much as the construction of the new medical center, completed in 1967. (Courtesy Del E. Webb Library, Loma Linda University.)

Five

GROWING PAINS

Citrus became the lifeblood of the Loma Linda area. Workers on the Frink Ranch are picking the valuable crop in this early 1900s photograph. (Courtesy Joe Frink.)

The *zanja* was the first reliable water supply for the Mission District, called at various times Old Town San Bernardino, Cottonwood Row, Redlands Junction, and Bryn Mawr. This section of the *zanja* in Redlands shows how the ditch might have looked in its primitive state, with cottonwoods and alders lining the banks.

Mill Creek drained a large area of the San Bernardino Mountains. Valley families enjoyed an outing at the source of their water and prosperity. (Courtesy Joe Frink.)

The *zanja* varied considerably in width and depth. This unidentified couple gazes on the quiet waters flowing through the Frink Ranch. (Courtesy Joe Frink.)

What better way to spend a Sunday afternoon than to drive a wagon partway through the *zanja* and become stuck, pile the wagon with family members, and then find a pony to make the picture even more comical. The writing on the wagon seems to be written with chalk. (Courtesy Joe Frink.)

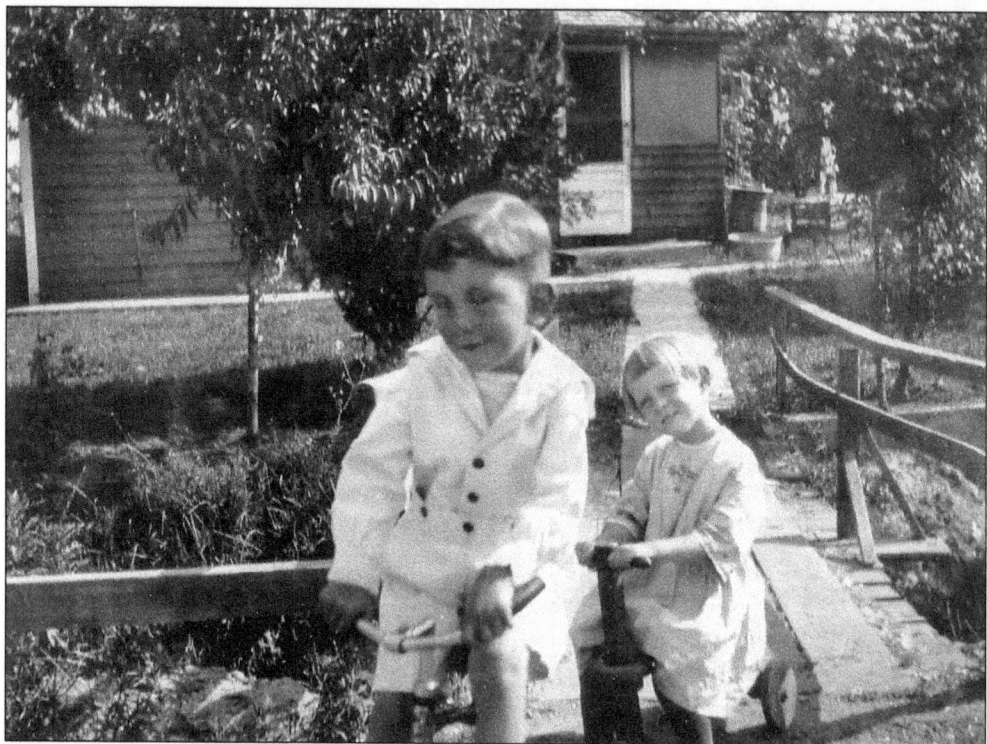

There was sometimes surplus water that passed all the way through the *zanja*, so an extension of the ditch was dug along Court Street, one of the first housing tracts off the Mound. Elmer Digneo and sister Lucille ride their trikes in front of the family home. (Courtesy Elmer Digneo.)

Ranchers realized the need for more water as the *zanja*'s meager supply was legally contested. This rig on the Frink Ranch would develop a well to supply water for their groves. (Courtesy Hale Paxton.)

The first wells in the area were artesian (water spurted up out of the ground) without need of a pump. The weight of the ground above the aquifer supplied the pressure. (Courtesy San Bernardino County Museum.)

Court Street maintained its own water company for many years after other local companies were consolidated under the college water system. (Courtesy Betty Stark.)

Jackie Unger drives her father's tractor, while sister Margie balances atop the load of hay. Unger's acreage was at the west end of Central, now University Avenue. (Courtesy Jackie Moncrieff.)

HOW ARE YOU FIXED FOR

HAY

You had better drop around and see us before it gets in the warehouse.

J. H. STEWART
13 E. CENTRAL AVE.

In a society partly fueled by hay, local growers kept the many horses and cows in the community well fed. J. H. Stewart, father of local landowner Willard Stewart, advertised in local papers. (Courtesy Michael Stewart.)

The orange growers of the Bryn Mawr area were well represented by this elaborately decorated buggy in the 1903 California State Fair parade in Sacramento. (Courtesy Joe Frink.)

This is a different kind of parade. A mule drag, usually used for hauling rocks and other heavy loads around the Frink Ranch, could be used to transport the ladies in a pinch. (Courtesy Joe Frink.)

The Bryn Mawr train station became a major shipper of local oranges, beginning with the first packing from Henry Fuller's barn in 1897. Before, oranges were hauled to one of the Redlands packinghouses for shipment. (Courtesy Joe Frink.)

The Bryn Mawr train station itself was used as a citrus packing shed from 1899 to 1902 until Pinkham and McKivett built the first packinghouse in Bryn Mawr. (Courtesy San Bernardino County Archives.)

It never hurts to invoke the name of Redlands as it was associated with Eastern money and elegant mansions. Bryn Mawr growers frequently used the name of Redlands on their packing crates, perhaps to connect the better known community with their product. (Courtesy City of Loma Linda.)

Oranges delivered by Mercury? Perhaps the intent of this citrus label was to imply that oranges from Bryn Mawr were delivered quickly to the East, which they were. (Courtesy City of Loma Linda.)

A substantial steel water tower on the south side of the Mound, seen here during construction, was a recognizable landmark from any spot in the valley. It was also a yearly target for Loma Linda Academy seniors to paint their graduation year. It was bedecked in patriotic colors in 1976 for the United States bicentennial. (Courtesy Del E. Webb Library, Loma Linda University.)

Loma Linda had to have its own dairy where Seventh-day Adventist health practices were applied to the resident chickens and cows. Vegetarian cows made milk for vegetarians. (Courtesy Del E. Webb Library, Loma Linda University.)

During the Great Depression, sanitarium employees could not be paid in cash but received tokens to buy fresh goods from the Mercantile. The farm kept the little community afloat during those hard times. (Courtesy Del E. Webb Library, Loma Linda University.)

When the School of Medicine moved into its own quarters west of the Mound, it was surrounded by the gardens and dairy farm. (Courtesy Del E. Webb Library, Loma Linda University.)

MODERN DAIRY

Cleanliness in the operation of a dairy was essential for safe milk. The dairy was located west of the present-day Anderson Street overpass. (Courtesy Del E. Webb Library, Loma Linda University.)

The dairy drive-in was a welcome stop for anyone in the community who needed basics: eggs, milk, bread, butter, cheese, and later, ice cream. (Courtesy Del E. Webb Library, Loma Linda University.)

The Cash and Carry Dairy Store was demolished to make way for the Anderson Street railroad overpass. (Courtesy Del E. Webb Library, Loma Linda University.)

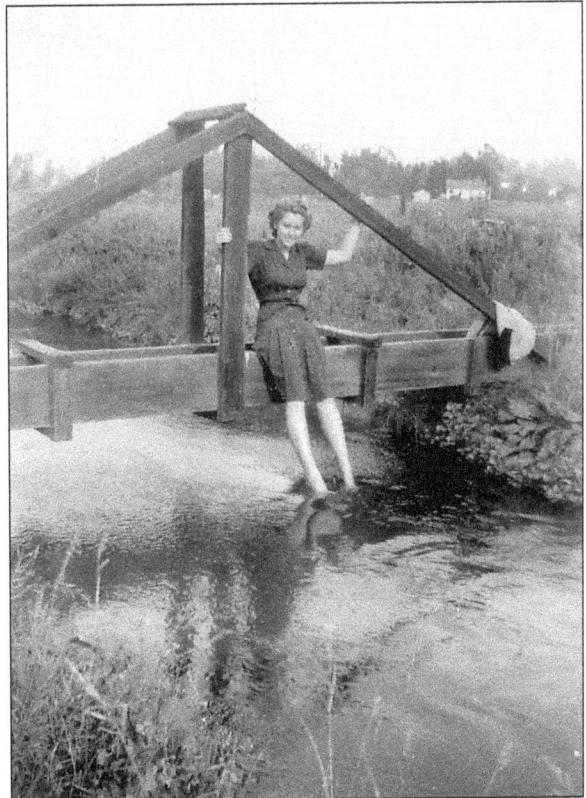

Matthew Gage needed water for the land he acquired in Riverside under the Desert Land Act. He dug a 12-mile canal to carry water from wells by the Santa Ana River in San Bernardino to his ranch. The canal skirted Van Unger's property and Jackie, Judge Unger's daughter, remembers swimming in the canal. "You could just swim fast enough to keep up with the current," she recalled. In this photograph, Jackie is sitting on one of the many small bridges that crossed the Gage Canal before it was covered. (Courtesy Jackie Moncrieff.)

The alders growing along the *zanja*, pictured here in 1917, were used by the Cram brothers to build the furniture in their water-powered furniture factory. (Courtesy San Bernardino County Archives.)

Fast-growing cottonwood trees were planted as fences along Mission Road, causing the little community to be known as Cottonwood Row. (Courtesy San Bernardino County Archives.)

Six

VILLAGE LIFE

John Capfer moved from Missouri around 1906 to provide blacksmithing to the new Seventh-day Adventist community of Loma Linda and its neighbors. His shop was built at the corner of Anderson and Redlands Boulevard, approximately where Baker's Tacos stands today. (Courtesy Jackie Moncrieff.)

This is a true "live and work" building in 1910 Loma Linda. The Capfers, including Miranda Capfer, seated in the second story, lived upstairs. (Courtesy Del E. Webb Library, Loma Linda University.)

John Capfer eats his breakfast. Note his cereal of choice—Kellogg's Toasted Corn Flakes. (Courtesy Del E. Webb Library, Loma Linda University.)

Florence Wical, shown at two months with her mother, Josie Berg, was the third baby of the new Seventh-day Adventist Mound community. She was born August 14, 1907, in one of the small cottages set up as a birthing room. (Courtesy Kenneth and Virginia Wical.)

While the cement-block Capfer blacksmith shop and home was being built, this tidy structure served as their temporary living quarters. (Courtesy Del E. Webb Library, Loma Linda University.)

The Capfers could provide more than blacksmithing as their fields also made hay. The family was one of the first in the area to own a car as well. (Courtesy Jackie Moncrieff.)

Digneo's OK Cash Market served the little community on Court Street. Mrs. Digneo, Mr. J. C. Digneo, Mrs. Johns, and Mr. James Johns stand in front of the neighborhood store. (Courtesy Elmer Digneo.)

Elmer Digneo's uncle, Henry Johnson, arrived in Loma Linda from Montana in the 1940s to take over the family store. He eventually operated the OK Cash Market, Ladera Market on San Juan Street, and another small store on Redlands Boulevard. (Courtesy Elmer Digneo.)

Within a few years the business center of Loma Linda would move south, away from the floods of the unruly San Timoteo Creek. At the time of this photograph, the area was all planted with citrus; it now holds the current Market and Medical Center. (Courtesy Del E. Webb Library, Loma Linda University.)

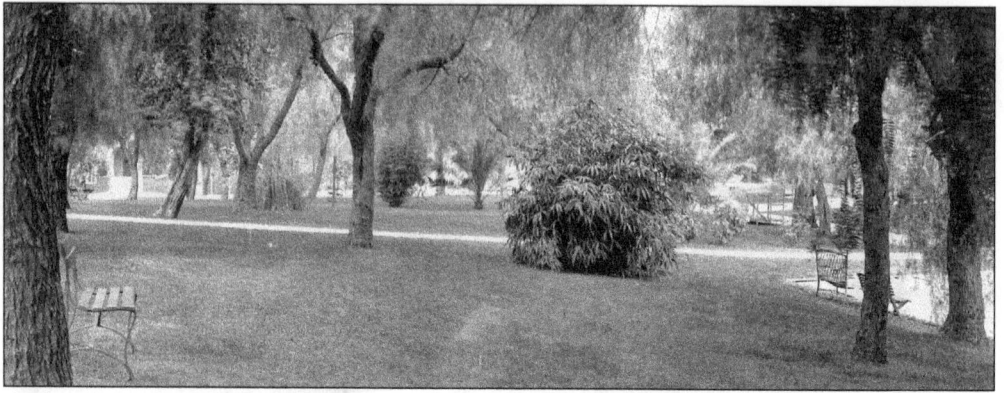

Anderson Street was once called Pepper Drive. The pepper trees, although beautiful, were messy and tended to shed large limbs. They gradually gave way to less troublesome trees and the street was renamed, perhaps for one of the original Mound City partners. (Courtesy Del E. Webb Library, Loma Linda University.)

The view south from the Mound was sparse in 1920 when this photograph from Mrs. Arthur Smith's album was taken. The land would gradually absorb Loma Linda Market and the new Medical Center. (Courtesy Del E. Webb Library, Loma Linda University.)

Many small but proud cottages lined Anderson Street, housing many employees of the sanitarium and the farm. Anderson is still a street of cottages. (Courtesy Del E. Webb Library, Loma Linda University.)

The bulk center of the market remains as popular as it was in 1953 when this photograph was taken. (Courtesy Del E. Webb Library, Loma Linda University.)

The College Market moved from place to place through the years but was always famous for a wide variety of healthy grains, robust bread, and many kinds of vegetarian meat substitutes. (Courtesy Del E. Webb Library, Loma Linda University.)

R. E. Emmerson operated his store on Central Avenue, now University, in the late 1920s. (Courtesy Del E. Webb Library, Loma Linda University.)

Ladera Heights was developed by William H. Howard around 1925. The Ladera Cash Market served the area around the "four gospels" streets: San Mateo, San Marcos, San Lucas, and San Juan. (Courtesy Del E. Webb Library, Loma Linda University.)

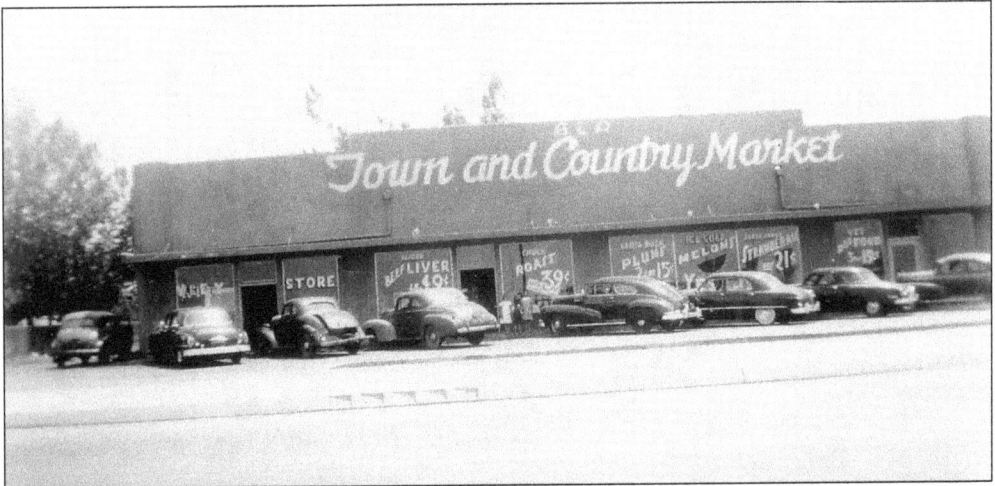

The Town and Country Market on Redlands Boulevard (once Colton Avenue) has had several transformations over the years. It has also been the Big 4 Market and now houses an antique mall. (Courtesy Betty Allen Stark and Vera Allen Coffer.)

No community with goats, chickens, sheep, cows, and horses would be complete without a feed store. In this photograph, taken around 1964, the store is about to move from Redlands Boulevard to Colton. Urbanization was no doubt responsible for declining business in Loma Linda. (Courtesy Loma Linda Fire Department.)

Southern Pacific Company

Los Angeles to Redlands, Riverside and San Bernardino

8 Daily	22 Daily	20 Daily	16 Daily	18 Daily	16 Daily	Mls	STATIONS	15 Daily	17 Daily	9 Daily	19 Daily	21 Daily	7 Daily
							READ DOWN / **READ UP**						
9.00pm	5.25pm	4.25pm	12.10pm	9.00am	8.05am	0	Lv .... Los Angeles .... Ar	8.50am	9.55am	12.55pm	4.45pm	6.50pm	10.50pm
9.22	5.45	4.43	12.32	9.18	8.26	6	.... Dolgeville	8.32	9.34	12.23am	4.26	6.31	10.16
....	5.49	4.49	....	9.21	8.29	7	.... Alhambra	8.29	9.29	....	4.21	6.27	....
....	5.52	4.53	....	9.25	8.32	10	.... San Gabriel	8.23	9.25	....	4.19	6.22	....
	6.10	5.05			8.46	17	.... Bassett	8.05			4.05		9.57
	6.29	....			9.04	24	.... Covina	7.50			3.47	5.55	
	6.43	....			9.15	29	.... San Dimas	7.41			3.37	5.46	
	6.49				9.21	31	.... Lordsburg	7.38			3.33	5.41	
9.42	6.58				9.31	34	Ar .... Pomona Lv	7.30		11.28	3.22	5.33	
		5.05pm		10.03am		17	Lv .... Bassett .... Ar		9.05am				9.57
10.20		5.31		10.13		30	.... Spadra		8.47				
		5.40	1.21pm			33	Ar .... Pomona Lv		8.41				9.30
	6.58				9.31am	34	.... Pomona						
	7.11				9.43	39	.... Chino	7.30am			3.22pm		
	7.23				9.57	39	.... Ontario	7.07			3.08		
				10.13am		34	.... Pomona				2.57		
10.39	7.23pm	5.70pm	1.39pm	10.25	9.57am	39	Lv .... Ontario .... Ar	7.07am	8.31am	11.28am	2.57pm	5.33pm	9.30
11.14	7.28	5.55		10.03		42	.... Cucamonga		8.24	11.13		5.22	9.15
	7.50	6.20	2.10	10.55	10.27	58	Ar .... Colton Lv	7.02	8.24		2.50		
		6.27	2.16	2.01pm	10.32		Lv .... Colton .... Ar	6.40	8.02	10.37	2.22	4.55	8.35pm
		6.33	2.23	2.10	10.39	62	.... Loma Linda		7.55	10.32	2.16	4.55	
		6.50	2.41	2.25	10.55	67	.... Redlands		7.47		2.10	4.48	
		7.08			11.10	70	Ar .... Crafton Lv		7.33	10.00	1.56	4.35	
	8.00pm	6.27pm	2.25pm	10.55am	10.37am	58	Lv .... Colton .... Ar	6.34am	7.50am	10.25am	2.09pm	4.52pm	7.50pm
	8.20	6.52	2.50	11.15	10.58	65	Ar .... Riverside Lv	6.20	7.30	10.07	1.50	4 28	7.25
	8.00pm	6.27pm	2.18pm	10.50am	10.37am	58	Lv .... Colton .... Ar	6.31am	7.50am	10.15am	2.05pm	4.47pm	7.50pm
	8.12	6.40	2.30	12.74	10.48	62	Ar .... San Bernardino Lv	6.20	7.38	10.05	1.55	4.35	7.40

The trains of the Southern Pacific, so vital for transportation of people and citrus in the past, are now considered a nuisance by some who live near the tracks and crossings. (Courtesy Del E. Webb Library, Loma Linda University.)

Although passengers can't find a station at Loma Linda, now freight trains still rumble through and occasionally stop, just as in this 1912 photograph. (Courtesy Del E. Webb Library, Loma Linda University.)

THE ONLY WAY TO SEE

Southern California

IS VIA THE

"Inside Track"

Special Train every morning from Los Angeles
(connecting from Pasadena) for

Riverside, Loma Linda and Redlands

Two hours and a half at *Riverside* for drive on far-famed Victoria and Magnolia Avenues, Two hours at *Redlands* for drive to Smiley Heights and over the McKinley Drive, where a view of the surrounding country is had, not excelled in Southern California. Returning via *Covina*, reaches Los Angeles early in the evening : : : : : : : : : :

A TRIP THROUGH THE ORANGE GROVES
AND FLOWERING GARDENS

Full Information at 261 South Spring Street
G. A. PARKYNS, A. G. F. and P. A.
N. R. MARTIN, D. P. A.

Southern Pacific

In answering advertisements please mention The Travelers' Blue Book.

Loma Linda was on the scenic route. (Courtesy Del E. Webb Library, Loma Linda University.)

67

The boom in car buying meant a necessary boom in car repairing. Van Unger, grandson of the village blacksmith and future judge, rented a little garage in the back of Roy Gaber's filling station and began a long career in automobile service. Roy and his wife, Nobie, stand by their station in 1931. (Courtesy Jackie Moncrieff.)

Loma Linda's banking affair was short but left behind a grand building that still stands today on Anderson Street. (Courtesy Del E. Webb Library, Loma Linda University.)

F. E. Corson, president of the board of the College of Medical Evangelists (now Loma Linda University), wanted safety and stability for the institution's money. The First National Bank of Loma Linda safeguarded the community's funds and issued U.S. currency from 1929 to 1935. (Courtesy Del E. Webb Library, Loma Linda University.)

The bank building now houses a barber shop and assorted university offices. (Courtesy Del E. Webb Library, Loma Linda University.)

The First National Bank issued $5, $10, and $20 bills. Original bills fetch high prices on online auctions today. Only about 10,000 bills were issued with "First National Bank of Loma Linda" imprinted on them. (Courtesy Del E. Webb Library, Loma Linda University.)

The corner of Anderson and University has lost the traffic triangle and Unger's service station seen in this 1942 photograph, but little else has changed. The building serving as Loma Linda market was the justice court from 1955 to 1980. A bank located there in the 1980s, and now the building houses Loma Linda University departments. (Courtesy Don Boadway.)

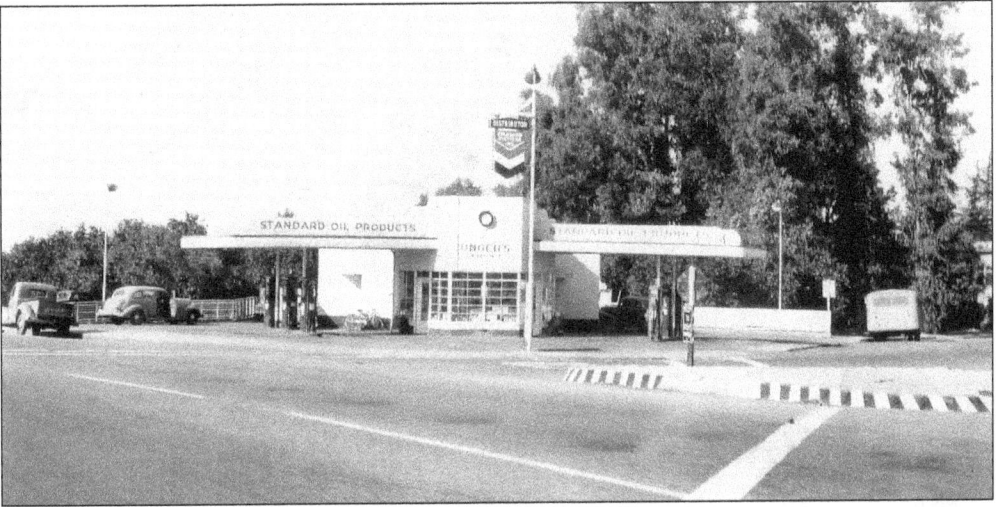

Van Unger's service station, seen from the First National Bank side of the corner in the 1940s, shows how much smaller the College of Medical Evangelists was in those years. Justice was served in a special room to the side. The same area seen in this picture now houses the Randall Visitors Center and the Del E. Webb Memorial Library. (Courtesy Jackie Moncrieff.)

Young Elmer Digneo plays with his dog under the watchful eye of his father, Joseph C. Digneo. Note the rain barrel at the corner of the house and the washtub and washing on the line, symbols of a simpler time when everyday housework took much time and energy. (Courtesy Elmer Digneo.)

This is the Digneo home in 1909. Mrs. Digneo wrote to her friend, Mrs. Proctor, in El Paso, Texas, stating "my 'hut' where we all live now. Hill mile south." (Courtesy Elmer Digneo.)

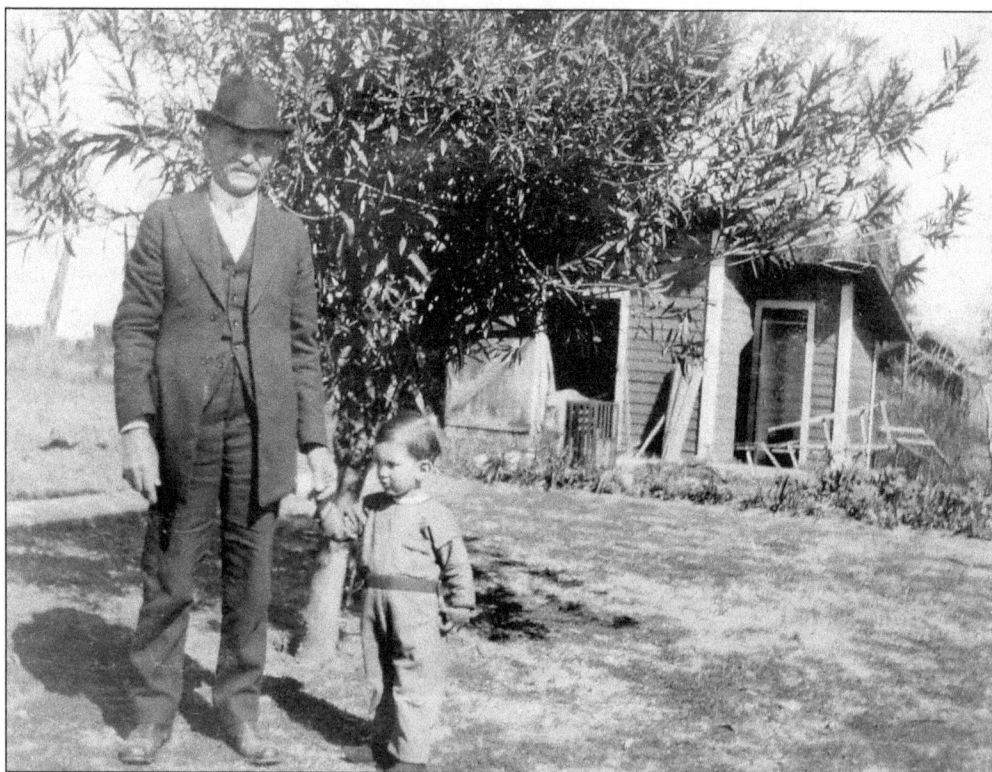

Grandfather Digneo, a skilled stonemason, emigrated from Italy around 1870 to help build St. Joseph Cathedral in Santa Fe, New Mexico. The job took 15 years. Young Elmer Digneo, future mayor, academy principal, and church organist, holds his grandfather's hand. (Courtesy Elmer Digneo.)

As the college expanded, Van Unger moved his business a few blocks west. The new station on University Avenue included space for a car showroom, and his home was built about the same time on the plowed field to the left. The Loma Linda Motel now stands on the site. (Courtesy Jackie Moncrieff.)

Getting married in a gas station? This happy couple, J. C. Gentry and Judge Unger's daughter Margarie, were actually married in church but posed for this shot near her dad's courtroom in the service station. (Courtesy Jackie Moncrieff.)

Judge Unger built this adobe hacienda on Central Avenue (now University Avenue) around 1946. At first he tried making his own bricks but then found a supplier of stabilized adobe bricks in Riverside. The home is still standing, although the bricks have been covered. (Courtesy Jackie Moncrieff.)

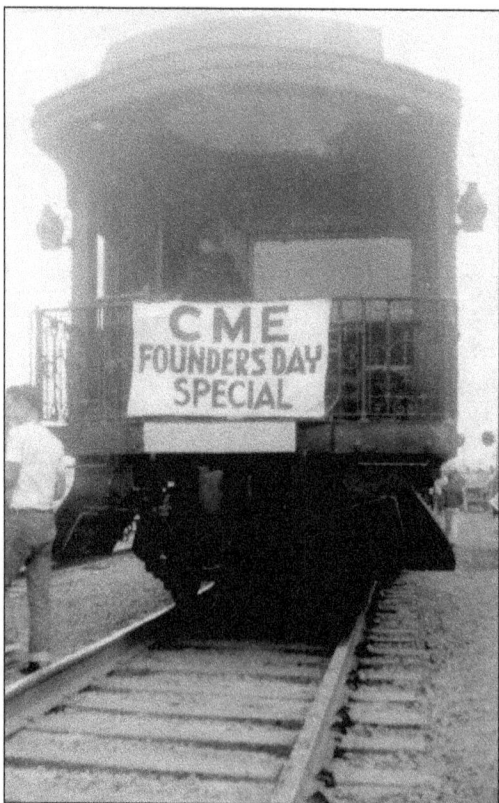

Founders Day in 1955 was a huge celebration, with a vintage train stop, participants in period clothing, and a parade. (Courtesy Kenneth and Virginia Wical.)

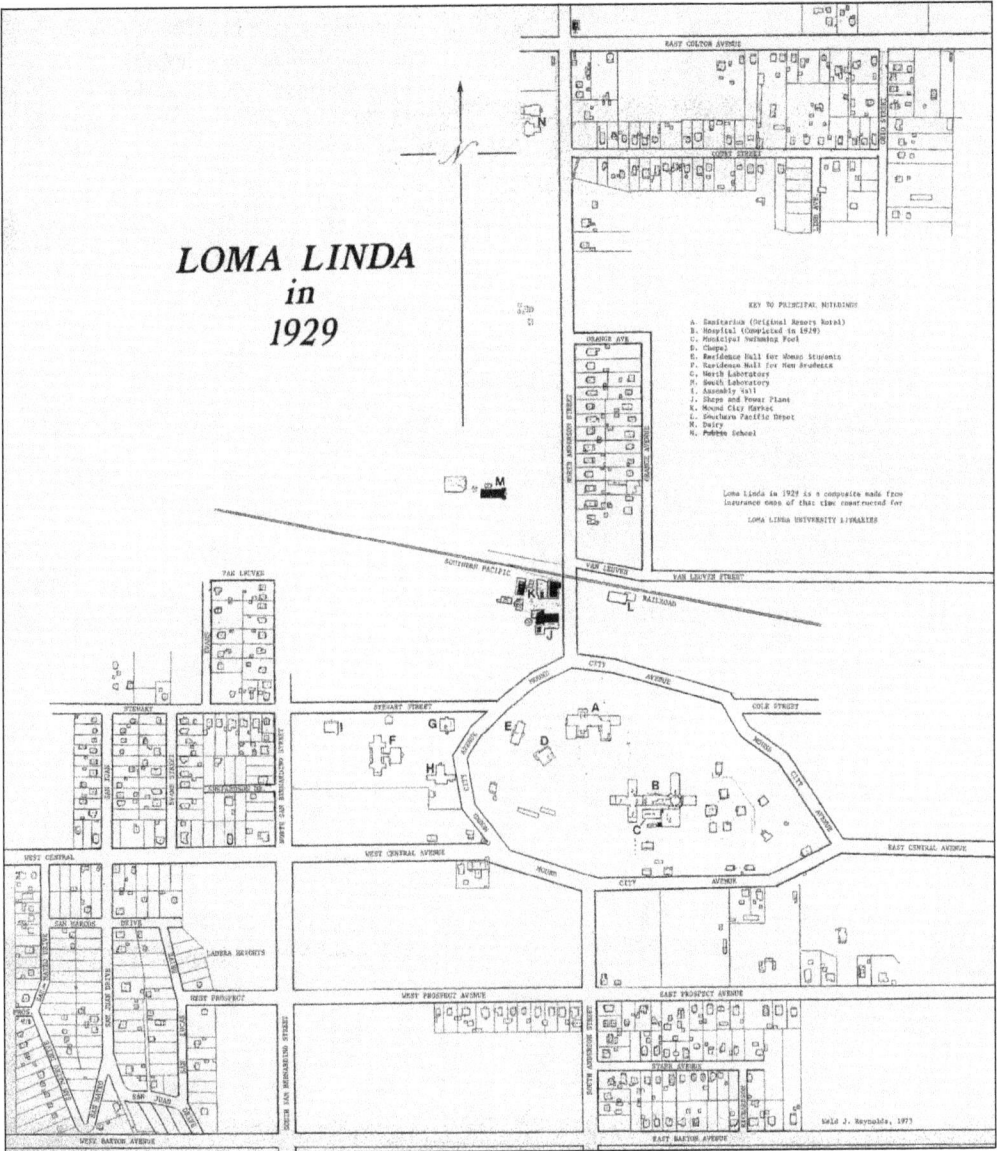

KEY TO PRINCIPAL BUILDINGS

A. Sanitarium (Original Resort Hotel)
B. Hospital (Completed in 1929)
C. Chapel
D. Municipal Swimming Pool
E. Residence Hall for Women Students
F. Residence Hall for Men Students
G. North Laboratory
H. South Laboratory
I. Assembly Hall
J. Shops and Power Plant
K. Mound City Market
L. Southern Pacific Depot
M. Dairy
N. Public School

Loma Linda in 1929 is a composite made from
insurance maps of that time reconstructed for

LOMA LINDA UNIVERSITY LIBRARIES

LOMA LINDA
in
1929

This 1973 map, created by Keld Reynolds, noted Loma Linda University historian, was from insurance maps that show the size and openness of the town in 1929; the boom was still to come. Visit the Loma Linda Chamber of Commerce to see a full-size copy of the map. (Courtesy Loma Linda Chamber of Commerce.)

75

This 1928 sheriff's notice announced the loss of substantial jewelry from one of the cottages. Jewelry was a rarity in a community where simple dress was the norm.

Circular Number 565 — MEMBER NATIONAL BUREAU OF IDENTIFICATION

Bureau of Identification
Sheriff's Office
San Bernardino, Calif.
JANUARY 12, 1928

BURGLARY

Cottage occupied by Mr. and Mrs. Duncan Smith, Loma Linda, entered through front door by pass key evening of December 29th, 1927, and the following articles taken:

2 gold baby rings with initial "N", one band cut into;

1 gent's gold ring, Masonic square and compass, ruby setting;

1 pearl necklace, joined together with silver rings;

1 souvenir brooch--British battleship and name "Vancouver" on it;

1 brooch setting of mother of pearl;

1 lady's gold pin with jade pendant;

1 pair gent's gold cuff links, Masonic square and compass on one side, initials "D. S." or "S" on other;

1 gold California stick pin made up of California gold coins;

1 baby's gold bracelet;

1 small bird's eye maple box;

4 or 5 dozen lady's and girl's handkerchiefs.

Notify **W. A. SHAY**, Sheriff.

O. W. B. Supt.
B. of I.   Or John Hetblack, Constable.

Redlands Boulevard was once Colton Avenue but was better known as "99," the main road from Palm Springs to Los Angeles. (Courtesy Del E. Webb Library, Loma Linda University.)

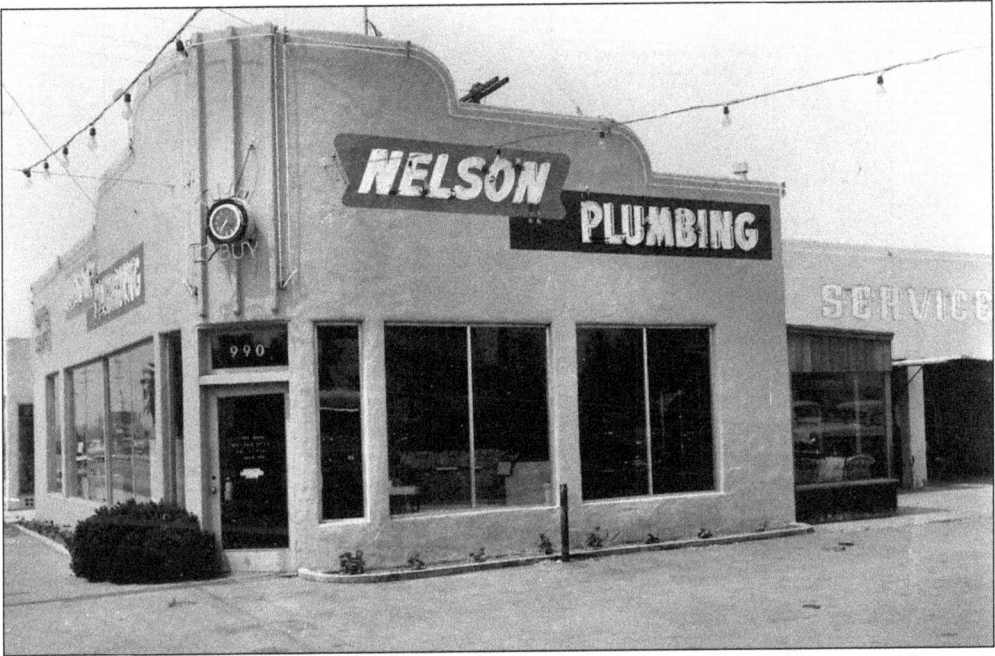

Nelson Plumbing served the community—as soon as indoor plumbing became the norm. (Courtesy Del E. Webb Library, Loma Linda University.)

Frank Boadway started cutting hair in 1946 in a building behind the bank. His son Don joined the business in 1958. Generations of men have been trimmed and groomed there, and it remains a social center of the community. (Courtesy Don Boadway.)

Loma Linda, Cal., **OCT 26 1918** 191...

Charges from

Loma Linda Sanitarium and Hospital

Owned and operated by the College of Medical Evangelists, a charitable corporation

TO

Miss Laura J. Sorensen

	DEBITS		CREDITS	
To 7 Days' Board, Room and Treatment at $ .... a week	24	00		
To ...... Days' Board, Room and Treatment at $ .... a week				
xxxx Meal Ticket	5	00		
Trays				
Examination				
Gastric Analysis				
Blood Test .... Urine Test				
X-ray				
Special Office Treatment Night call		25		
Special Electrical Treatment				
Extra Bath-room Treatment				
Nose, Throat, Eye and Ear .... Glasses	25	00		
Wheel Chair				
Head Shampoo" .... Special Massage		50		
Nurse		87		
Laundry				
Stamps .... Express .... Newspaper				
Telephone and Telegram		25		
Automobile .... Garage				
Supplies		25		
Surgery				
Operating Room .... Anaesthetic				
Cash				
Amount for week	56	12		
Balance	29	55		
Total	85	67		
Balance				

A 1918 sanitarium bill was paid in cash, without insurance, HMOs, or any other complications.

Seven

FIRES, FROSTS, AND FLOODS

This was Loma Linda's first fire engine. The 1917 Seagrave sported a massive chain drive, solid rubber tires, and moved like a snail. (Courtesy Loma Linda Fire Department.)

The Seagrave machine wasn't doing the pumping in this staged photograph, it was just a fine chance to dress up and show how the volunteers protected the community. The fire department began to organize in 1922, but official recognition came in 1926. (Courtesy Loma Linda Fire Department.)

A brand-new Model AA Ford truck chassis was shipped from Detroit to Loma Linda via railroad flatcar in 1931. The firemen transferred the major equipment from the Seagrave truck to the new Ford. Even the bell, spotlight, and running lights made the move. The homemade Ford fire truck can still be seen at the fire department museum, and it often rolls through town for the Loma Linda community parade in October. (Courtesy Loma Linda Fire Department.)

The chemical tanks were required for special kinds of fire-fighting needed around a hospital and laboratories. Reaction between acid and carbonated water in the tanks created a stream of carbon dioxide. (Courtesy Loma Linda Fire Department.)

By 1946, the fire department had three trucks and several volunteer companies. Chief Francis Dinsmore led the department. Equipment was housed at the college engineering/power plant facility. (Courtesy Loma Linda Fire Department.)

Fire Department

In case of fire Dial 2710, which is the Loma Linda operator. Give your name and location of fire by street and number, talking slowly and distinctly so operator can copy.

Signals given by siren blow for one-half minute duration. Districts as follows:

District No. 1—Sanitarium Hill, siren sounds intermittently every ten seconds.
District No. 2—College Division...Two (2) Whistles
District No. 3—South Side of Hill..Three (3) Whistles
District No. 4—West Side, Ladera...Four (4) Whistles
District No. 5—North Anderson, Court St., Colton Ave.......Five (5) Whistles
District No. 6—Van Luvan and Poplar Streets.......................Six (6) Whistles
District No. 7—Cole Street and Benton Ave...............................Seven 7) Whistles

Turn off all sprinklers and irrigation water when you hear the fire alarm.
Two short whistles for fire out given only in day time. (FIREMEN ONLY SHOULD ANSWER CALLS.)

POLICE DEPT.—	SAN BERNARDINO	2101
	REDLANDS	3141
SHERIFF—	SAN BERNARDINO	6826
AMBULANCE	REDLANDS	6161
STATE FORESTRY FIRE DEPT.—LOMA LINDA		2922

Fire cards were available in local stores and the same information was printed in the 1945 community directory. By listening to the very loud siren, volunteer firemen knew exactly where to go to meet their fire company.

When the main building of Loma Linda Academy burned in 1948, most records and documents were lost. There was not enough money to rebuild the whole facility, so new buildings were erected on the original foundations. (Courtesy Jackie Moncrieff.)

The loss of the academy was a huge blow, but school went on. Classes were taught in elementary school classrooms in double sessions. Staff and students soldiered on until the buildings were rebuilt. (Courtesy Jackie Moncrieff.)

The whole fire department "family" gathered for this portrait in 1929. (Courtesy Loma Linda Fire Department.)

The best ladder practice location in town was the side of the college power plant, conveniently the same place where the trucks were kept. The other side of the building was used for rappelling practice. (Courtesy Loma Linda Fire Department.)

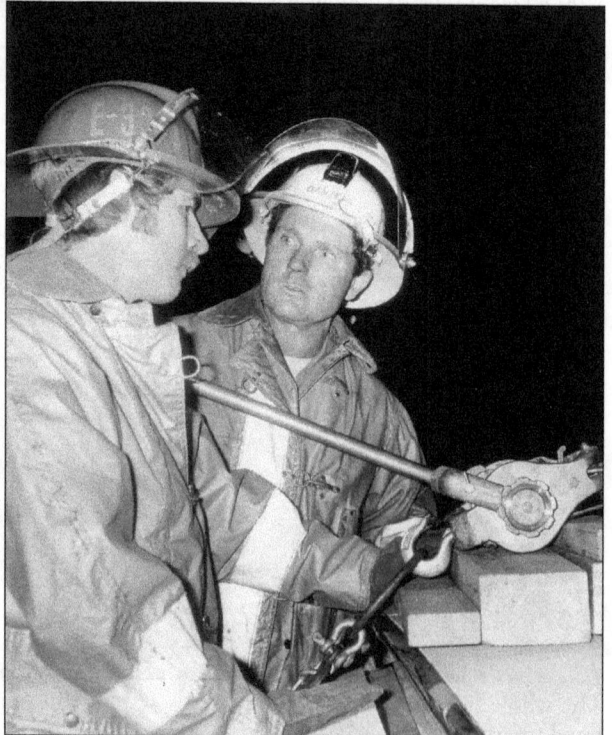

Capt. Peter Hills and Fireman Ernie Daniel contemplate the best way to use a winch in this rescue drill in 1974. (Courtesy Loma Linda Fire Department.)

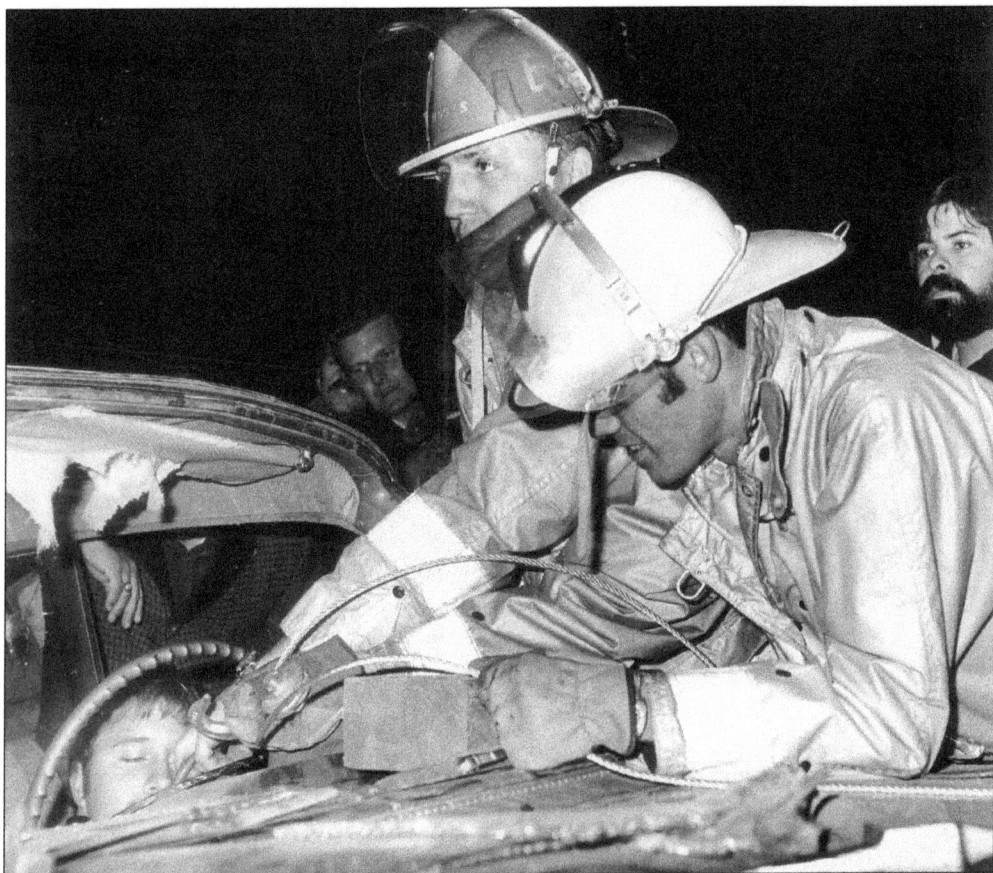

Capt. Gene Brooks and Fireman Bob Fuller try to extricate "victim" Captain Hills from a smashed car in this 1974 rescue drill. (Courtesy Loma Linda Fire Department.)

The fire department had to buy new equipment to keep up with the new Medical Center and Veterans Administration Hospital. By 1974, there were more trucks than space, so a truck had to be stored every night in a nearby service station. A new station seemed an urgent need. (Courtesy Loma Linda Fire Department.)

The Stewart farmhouse, an elegant Victorian, was a total loss in 1972. Like many other historic homes and barns in town, it burned under suspicious circumstances. (Courtesy Michael Stewart.)

This spectacular blaze was set by firefighters while training at Cone Camp in 1977. (Courtesy Loma Linda Fire Department.)

While the city council debated the cost, site, and materials for a new fire station, the equipment barely fit into available space. (Courtesy Loma Linda Fire Department.)

The hills behind Loma Linda burned in 1979. Retardant-dropping airplanes came the rescue to combat this Reche Canyon blaze. (Courtesy Loma Linda Fire Department.)

A photograph taken at night of a fire in San Timoteo Canyon in 1979 reveals tornado-like plumes of flame that are both frightening and beautiful. Loma Linda stands proudly along hundreds of acres of wildland to the south that have burned repeatedly over the years. (Courtesy Loma Linda Fire Department.)

In the most expensive fire in Loma Linda's history, the top floor of Risley Hall on the college campus burned in 1964 because of an overheated lighting ballast. The top floor was removed and the building was re-roofed as a single-story building. (Courtesy Del E. Webb Library, Loma Linda University.)

A white blanket covers the Frink Adobe. Although snow was an exciting diversion for local children, low temperatures could doom the entire year's citrus crop. (Courtesy Joe Frink.)

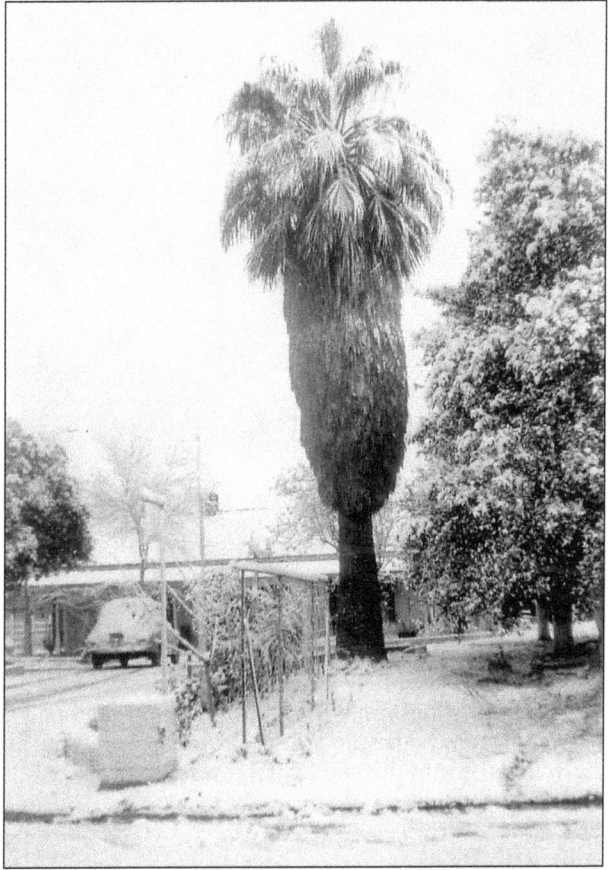

This snow was heavy and wet, not like the light dusting seen in recent decades. It coated everything, even the orange trees and power lines. (Courtesy Joe Frink.)

Ankle-deep snow in 1949 worried citrus growers. These workers on the Frink Ranch are carrying smudge-pot lighters. Smudge pots cast an oil-fired pall over the whole valley during a freeze, blackening cars, homes, and the entire landscape. Wind machines were also used to keep freezing air from settling in the groves. (Courtesy Joe Frink.)

This 1949 view of snow in Loma Linda shows evidence of plowing along Anderson Street near the present-day Loma Linda Market and Post Office. (Courtesy Del E. Webb Library, Loma Linda University.)

Ethel Casey, wife of Loma Linda postmaster Ira Casey, is pictured here with her children after a snowstorm in 1921. (Courtesy Elmer Digneo.)

Major floods in 1916 and 1927 inundated the "lowlands" of Loma Linda. This photograph, taken from the Court Street side of the Anderson Street Bridge, shows the devastation. Power poles, railroad ties, whole trees, and even cars regularly floated down San Timoteo Creek during a flood. (Courtesy Elmer Digneo.)

When the creek filled completely with silt in 1927, water washed across the landscape with brutal fury. (Courtesy Elmer Digneo.)

In another image of the 1927 flood, Anderson Street was completely washed out north of the railroad tracks. The Loma Linda Mercantile Store and power plant are just visible beyond the Southern Pacific freight train. (Courtesy Elmer Digneo.)

The 1927 flood proved that the San Timoteo Creek had tremendous power to choose its own course. This photograph was taken from the west end of Van Leuven Avenue. Houses in the distance flank Poplar Street. (Courtesy Elmer Digneo.)

The Loma Linda Academy buildings were originally on the north side of the creek, about where KB Subs stands today. The 1927 flood left a mess. (Courtesy Elmer Digneo.)

The home of Arthur Nelson had been known as the Dew Drop Inn before the 1916 flood. (Courtesy Del E. Webb Library, Loma Linda University.)

This is another view of the Anderson Street Bridge after the 1916 flood. (Courtesy Del E. Webb Library, Loma Linda University.)

The 1969 flood took one human life, but this dog was rescued. This photograph was taken at Court and Ohio Streets. (Courtesy Del E. Webb Library, Loma Linda University.)

The Poplar Street neighborhood near the creek never fully recovered from the 1969 flood. (Courtesy Del E. Webb Library, Loma Linda University.)

Not even the mighty Southern Pacific was exempt from the San Timoteo Canyon floods. Washouts like this sent hundreds of railroad ties down the creek to batter the bridges at Beaumont Avenue, Barton Road, Mountain View Avenue, and Anderson Street. The Van Leuven crossing was a dip in the road for many years that was impassable during most rainstorms. (Courtesy San Bernardino County Museum.)

When houses were built too close to the creek, or the creek changed course, things could get pretty grim. (Courtesy San Bernardino County Museum.)

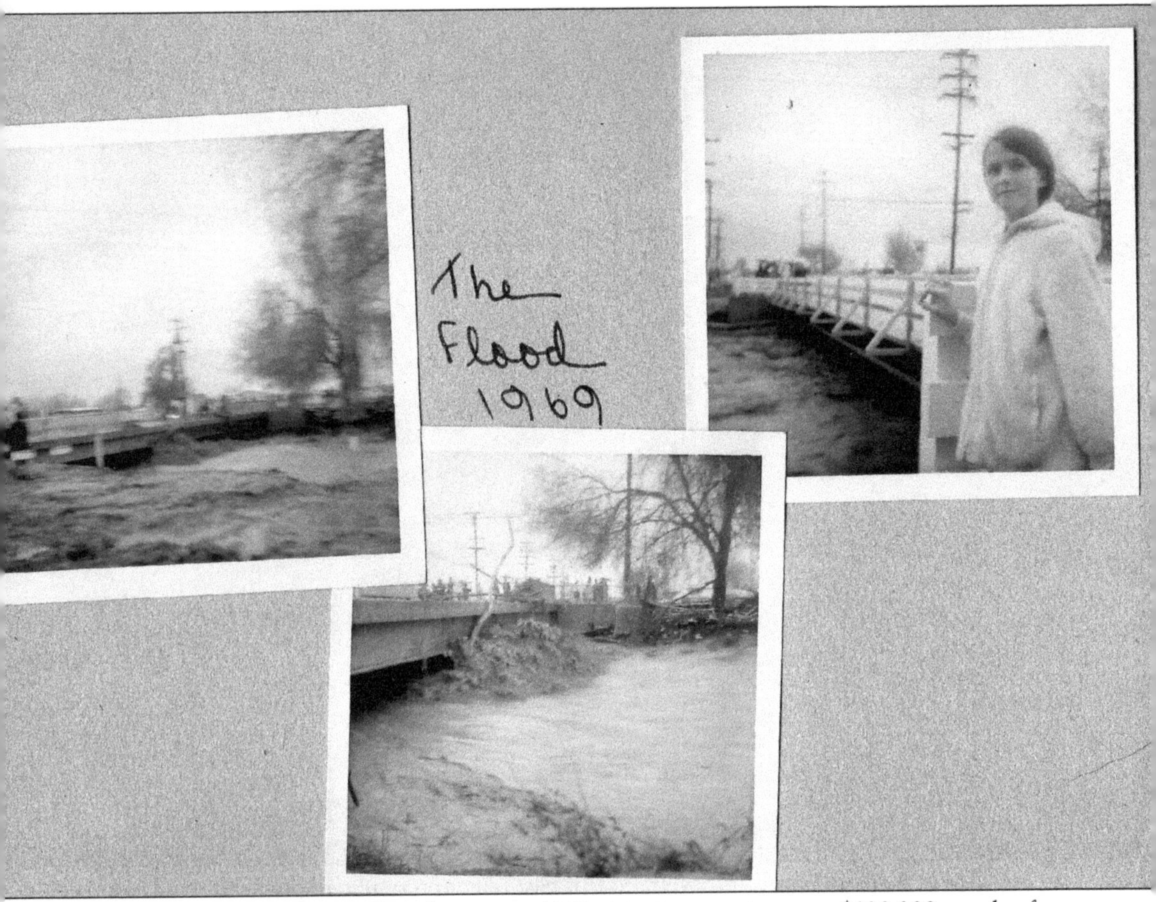
The Flood
1969

The San Timoteo Creek overflowed again in 1969, this time causing over $100,000 worth of damage to Loma Linda Academy alone. Once again the lowlands became a sea of mud. (Courtesy Michael Stewart.)

The Army Corps of Engineers developed this vast retention system to protect Loma Linda and areas downstream from the raging San Timoteo Creek. The project got an immediate workout with the rains of 2004. Silt filled the retention basins but stayed put. (Courtesy Dick Wiley.)

Eight

LEARNING AND LEISURE

The Mission School of 1904, midway down Mission Road on the south side, was a far cry from the simple slab structure that the Van Leuvens helped build in 1854. Several versions of Mission School were built, each one a little bigger and more sophisticated. This school building had a large community hall upstairs for dances and other programs. (Courtesy Hale Paxton.)

This two-room version of Mission School was third in succession. Built in the 1880s, it was moved across the creek after the new school was built in 1904. It became the community hall for the Bryn Mawr School and is now the youth room and fellowship hall of the Romanian Seventh-day Adventist Church on Mayberry Street and Whittier Avenue. (Courtesy Redlands Unified School District.)

Mission School District.

Monthly Report of

Lizzie Frink

8th Grade.

For the School Year beginning *Sept. 20, 1899*

MONTHS	1	2	3	4	5	6	7	8	9
Reading & Literature	9	60	90						
Language	9	8	73	83	88	83	90		
Grammar	7	7	53	80	90	92	99		
Spelling	8	8	96	90	99	99			
Arithmetic	P	7	30	50	66	96	73		
Geography						17	90		
History	7	7	70	83	100	-			
Science						17	89		
Drawing				80	85	95			
Writing			91	90	92	92	92		
Music		7	100	100	85				
Excused Absences	6½	2	3	0	0	0	0		
Unexcused Absences	0	0	0	0	0	0	0		
Times Tardy	0	0	6	0	0	0	0		
Deportment	7	8	8	98	98				

RANK:—90 to 100, Excellent; 80 to 90, Good; 70 to 80, Fair; 60 to 70, Poor; below 60, Very Poor.

7/m 96.6+

Frances R. Saunders Teacher.
93.3
Rank's 4-6-1-4

Lizzie Frink, a Mission Road native, earned good marks in eighth grade at the 1880 Mission School in 1899. (Courtesy Hale Paxton.)

Mission School teachers and students took their pioneer heritage very seriously. These students are acting out the westward movement with lifelike horse replicas and a covered wagon. (Courtesy Redlands Unified School District.)

Many of the students' grandparents and great-grandparents were real covered-wagon pioneers. The 1937 Mission School was a center of pioneer studies, with log cabins built in classrooms and numerous hands-on activities. (Courtesy Redlands Unified School District.)

San Bernardino County
Public • •
Schools

THE U. S. S. MAINE

Bryn Mawr California, May 30th, 1898.

This is to Certify, that Charlie Brown
is a contributor to the fund for the purpose of building a
battleship, to take the place of the "Maine" destroyed in
Havana Harbor, Feb. 15, 1898.

Margaret McMiggean

Superintendent.

ORDERED BY THE
COUNTY BOARD OF EDUCATION
MAY 21, 1898.

Francis R Saunders Principal.

Teacher.

When the USS *Maine* was destroyed in Havana Harbor in 1898, Charlie Brown, a student at Mission School, contributed an undisclosed amount of money for its replacement. (Courtesy Michael Stewart.)

Built in 1905 in Bryn Mawr, this school was a part of the system of "Mexican" schools common in California at the turn of the century. Gov. Earl Warren outlawed segregated schools in 1947. By that time, Apollonia Rey, Bryn Mawr PTA president, had successfully petitioned the Redlands Unified School District to integrate the new Mission School. This school closed in 1943 but, as you shall see, had much more life left in it. (Courtesy San Bernardino County Archives.)

The old Bryn Mawr School became the home of the Sacred Heart Roman Catholic Church. Mass was held weekly and the building continued as the cultural center of the community. (Courtesy Nellie Rodriguez.)

By 1951, when this picture was taken, Mission School on California Street was fully integrated. Mrs. Fernanda Cruz's class is pictured. (Courtesy Betty Stark.)

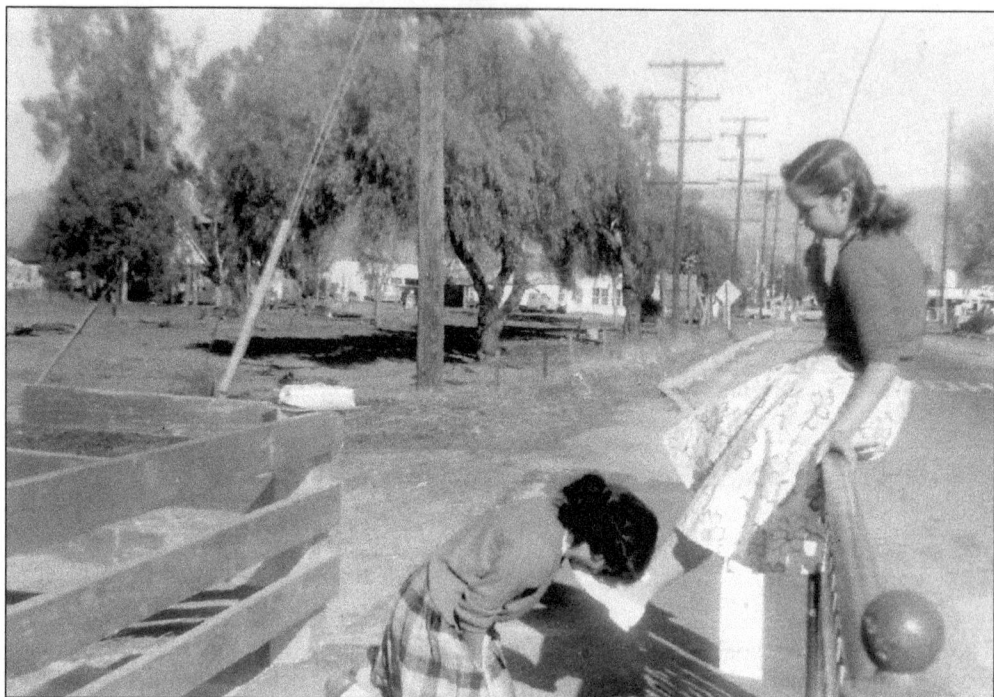

It was 1957 and "slave day" at Mission School. Betty Allen and her "servant" for the day, Irene Lopez, wait on the Anderson Street Bridge for the school bus. (Courtesy Betty Stark.)

The first church school on the Mound was a tent. It lasted until a bull, enraged by flapping canvas, destroyed it. Students met in this assembly hall in 1906 until a separate school could be built. (Courtesy Del E. Webb Library, Loma Linda University.)

Loma Linda Academy's main building is pictured just before the big fire in 1948. (Courtesy Jackie Moncrieff.)

Here is Loma Linda Academy after the fire. The new building mostly followed the old foundations, with minor changes in the façade. (Courtesy Loma Linda Fire Department.)

Miss Wallace, an academy teacher, directs basketball class while the academy is being rebuilt in the background. (Courtesy Jackie Moncrieff.)

REFLECTIONS

VOLUME I, NUMBER 1   Loma Linda Academy Alumni and Friends   APRIL 1979

Ted Dawson — the five-foot, five-inch giant

Ted Dawson is a big little man. For 23 years he worked behind the scenes at Loma Linda Academy, quietly doing his job...and more. People thought he was the custodian. In reality, however, he was (and still is) an organizer. His main goal in life is to "get the job done." And that job is Christian education.

Although not an "educator" himself, he has done everything possible to promote Christian education, from building churches and buying school buses to paying the tuition of hundreds of students, probably over three hundred.

"I couldn't begin to count them," he says. "I never thought about keeping records. It's just a matter of 'doing the job.'"

At one time he was supporting at least 30 students in academy and college. "I don't know how we did it," he says. Some of "his" students are now physicians, nurses, physical therapists, and dietitians. One is a minister.

How could the Dawsons afford such a financial burden? "Oh, we couldn't afford that," he says. "We asked for donations." In seeking financial help for needy students, Dawson arranged for donors to get a tax deductible receipt.

"The Lord has blessed considerably," he says. "He impressed people to give and gave us strength to keep going."

How does Dawson receive strength? "Every morning we follow the program of submitting to the Lord," he says. "He keeps you busy. You don't have to look around for a job."

By 1977, Dawson had solicited well over $100,000 for needy students.

Although "money is harder to get now than it used to be," Dawson continues to help needy students. This year he is supporting nine such students: "two in Mexico, three at La Sierra, one in Washington, D.C., and three in Texas." This year's effort will cost $18,700. "I still have to raise $4,000," he says. "We encourage the students to work for their room and board, but we pay the tuition."

Because of his generosity and continued commitment to Loma Linda Academy and its students, Dawson received special honors—and a standing ovation—at the homecoming banquet in November.

Ted Dawson poses with Marjorie Reynolds Schaefer, '63, editor of the 1963 LOMASPHERE that was dedicated to him. Dawson and his wife have raised more than $100,000 to help needy students obtain a Christian education.

The 1963 LOMASPHERE was dedicated to Ted Dawson.

Ted and Lila Dawson gave to the community in many ways. This 1979 article from the *Loma Linda Academy Alumni* newsletter details how the Dawsons raised over $100,000 to make it possible for students to attend church schools and college. A small park at the corner of Court Street and Anderson Street honors their dedication. (Courtesy Loma Linda Fire Department.)

106

The Loma Linda class of 1938 poses with their class sweaters. The sweaters cost $15 each, a huge investment at the time. (Courtesy Elmer Digneo.)

The Loma Linda Academy juniors of 1947 showed a more casual side than earlier generations. (Courtesy Jackie Moncrieff.)

Miss Helen Johnson's third- and fourth-grade class at Loma Linda Elementary School in 1939 apparently had 40 students—and a dog. Miss Johnson was one of the best-loved of those years, teaching creatively and energetically. (Courtesy Jackie Moncrieff.)

It looks to be Halloween at the Frink Adobe. This picture is undated but is one of the earliest known photographs of the historic home. Note the wooden porch, which was later replaced with concrete. (Courtesy Joe Frink.)

Ruth and Milton Frink pose in front of Bahr's Store in Bryn Mawr. The Auburn car was built when America hadn't yet finalized having the steering wheel on the left side of the car. Milton loved fast machines and dogs, both of which appear here—although Ruth was the greatest love of his life. (Courtesy Joe Frink.)

"Fuzzy" Van Leuven follows the school bus in his Model T roadster. Norman Hinckley is following in his own Ford. (Courtesy Hale Paxton.)

R. M. Van Leuven's "Fast Ford" often raced at Banning and Ascot. Is this crowd waiting for a race to start? The public is encouraged to help identify the unique building in this photograph in the Frink family collection. (Courtesy Joe Frink.)

Yourself and Ladies are cordially invited to

A Social Dance

On Tuesday Evening, May 6, 1902,

at

Hinckley's Hall, Bryn Mawr,

on the occasion of the wedding of

Miss Lizzie Frink

to

Mr. Leonard Bahr.

Before the new Mission School was built in 1904, community dances and special events were held in Hinckley's Hall, a pavilion on the Mission Road Hinckley Ranch. (Courtesy Hale Paxton.)

Milton's love of fast machines extended to his motorcycles, including this two-cylinder Indian, with Kenneth Frink on the jump seat. (Courtesy Joe Frink.)

Hale Paxton sits behind the wheel of R. M. Van Leuven's Rajo 2. This fast Ford was driven in many races at local racetracks. (Courtesy Hale Paxton.)

Loma Linda had a seasonal surplus of water—during floods—but few lakes or ponds. Students from Loma Linda Elementary School and Academy took their usual end-of-year picnic trip to Fairmont Park in Riverside. (Courtesy Elmer Digneo.)

The parade in 1955 was in honor of 50 years of sanitarium operation. The parade is rounding the curve of Anderson Street near Central, now known as University Avenue. (Courtesy Loma Linda Fire Department.)

Judge Unger and companions joined the community parade in 1960. They are heading west on Prospect Avenue behind the Loma Linda Market. (Courtesy Jackie Moncrieff.)

The college swimming pool was open to the community during the summer. Generations of children paid their quarter to cool off. Here Mervilyn Adams earns the respect and admiration of the swimmers below by bravely taking on the high-diving platform. (Courtesy Jackie Moncrieff.)

Inventive children used skates, boards, and sometimes orange-packing crates to make their own scooters, long before the availability of manufactured skateboards and scooters. (Courtesy Jackie Moncrieff.)

Students at Loma Linda Academy were inspired by a Saturday night gymnastics performance, and balancing became the newest fad. Artis Gifford takes on the high wire around 1947. (Courtesy Jackie Moncrieff.)

The whole community turned out to the Tri-city Airport in 1928 to see the first tri-motor plane land there. (Courtesy Elmer Digneo.)

Summer camp in Idylwild was a tradition for young people in Loma Linda. These happy campers are headed off in the Lynwood Academy bus to Senior Camp in 1947. (Courtesy Jackie Moncrieff.)

Hulda Crooks was the ambassador of fitness. She took up mountain climbing later in life than most people, climbing Mount Whitney more than 40 times, traversing up more than 200 western peaks, and tackling Mount Fuji. A steep hillside park at the south end of Mountain View Avenue commemorates her courage and determination. (Courtesy Elmer Digneo.)

Ruth Weed Frink and Milton Joseph Frink, married on June 18, 1913, share a tender moment on a porch swing. No fast cars or motorcycles are anywhere in sight. (Courtesy Joe Frink.)

Nine

A COMMUNITY OF FAITH

The Campus Hill Church of Seventh-day Adventists, built in 1937, replaced the chapel of 1910. It is currently undergoing extensive restoration and a planned addition. (Courtesy Loma Linda Fire Department.)

The Chapel on the Hill was the first separate church building to serve the sanitarium community of Seventh-day Adventists. The ramp to the left allowed patients in wheelchairs to be taken directly to the balcony. When the building was demolished in 1938, several of the curved pews made their way into the choir room of the Campus Hill Church. Wood from the church was salvaged by W. F. Hardt and S. P. S. Edwards to build houses on Evans and Ohio Streets. (Courtesy Elmer Digneo.)

On January 4, 1942, Elmer Digneo played organ for the Seventh-day Adventist radio program *Voice of Prophecy*. The program featured pastor H. M. S. Richards, seated at the left. Music was provided by the quartet King's Heralds. (Courtesy Elmer Digneo.)

118

Which came first, the tower or the church? The new College Church, now known as the University Church of Seventh-day Adventists, opened its new doors in 1960. (Courtesy Del E. Webb Library, Loma Linda University.)

The University Church, under construction in 1959, has just gone through a major renovation in 2004 and 2005. (Courtesy Del E. Webb Library, Loma Linda University.)

The University Church of Seventh-day Adventists, completed in 1960, provided a home for the college church congregation, which had been meeting in Burden Hall for several years. (Courtesy Loma Linda Fire Department.)

The Youth of the Sacred Heart Roman Catholic Church in Bryn Mawr pose in this photograph from the 1940s. Fr. Peter Barron, in vestments to the right of the youth, led the congregation. Fred Ramos, historical commissioner, is in the back row, third from the right. (Courtesy Nellie Rodriguez.)

This little chapel housed a shrine to Our Lady of the Citrus. A frozen citrus crop was a devastating blow to the community, and the Bryn Mawr community believed this shrine protected their livelihood. (Courtesy Nellie Rodriguez.)

The Roman Catholic congregation broke ground for their new church in 1959 on land donated by Otillia Van Leuven. (Courtesy St. Joseph the Worker Catholic Church.)

St. Joseph the Worker Catholic Church interior is pictured shortly after completion in 1960. (Courtesy St. Joseph the Worker Catholic Church.)

Seventh-day Adventists are conscientious objectors, refusing to bear arms but willing to serve in the armed forces in medical units. This photograph, taken about 1944, shows the Junior Medical Cadet Corp in marching drill. (Courtesy Jackie Moncrieff.)

Ten

CELEBRATING THE PAST

This stone arch and carriage house have come to be the symbol of historic preservation on Mission Road. They will form the entryway into the future Heritage Park.

Before the Romanian Seventh-day Adventist Church members began renovation in 1999, the 1888 Mission School building looked beyond rescue. It now houses the fellowship hall and youth center of the church.

The Cole House on Redlands Boulevard will probably be moved to a place in the Heritage Park on Mission Road.

The giant Army Corps of Engineers project in San Timoteo required the removal of the World War II surplus Bailey Bridge from Beaumont Avenue. The bridge had been acquired for the community through the efforts of county supervisor Wesley Break after the war. (Courtesy Dick Wiley.)

The bridge sections were disassembled and have been placed across San Timoteo Creek as pedestrian bridges. (Courtesy Dick Wiley.)

This structure, now known as the Curtis-Fisk House, awaits lowering onto its new foundation beside the *zanja*. It was first the home of Robert Curtis, Cottonwood Row native and Horticultural Commission secretary. Later it became the home of O. J. and Della Fisk. O. J. Fisk helped found the San Bernardino County Museum Association with Dr. Gerald Smith, and the Fisks contributed generously to the construction of the San Bernardino County Museum. The relocated home may become the headquarters of Loma Linda's own historical society.

The old Bryn Mawr school shines as the current home of the Romanian Church of Seventh-day Adventists. Major renovations were done by the church members themselves in 2000.

The Allen Break Estate stands grandly beside Hulda Crooks Park, where it reminds citizens of the community's citrus heritage.

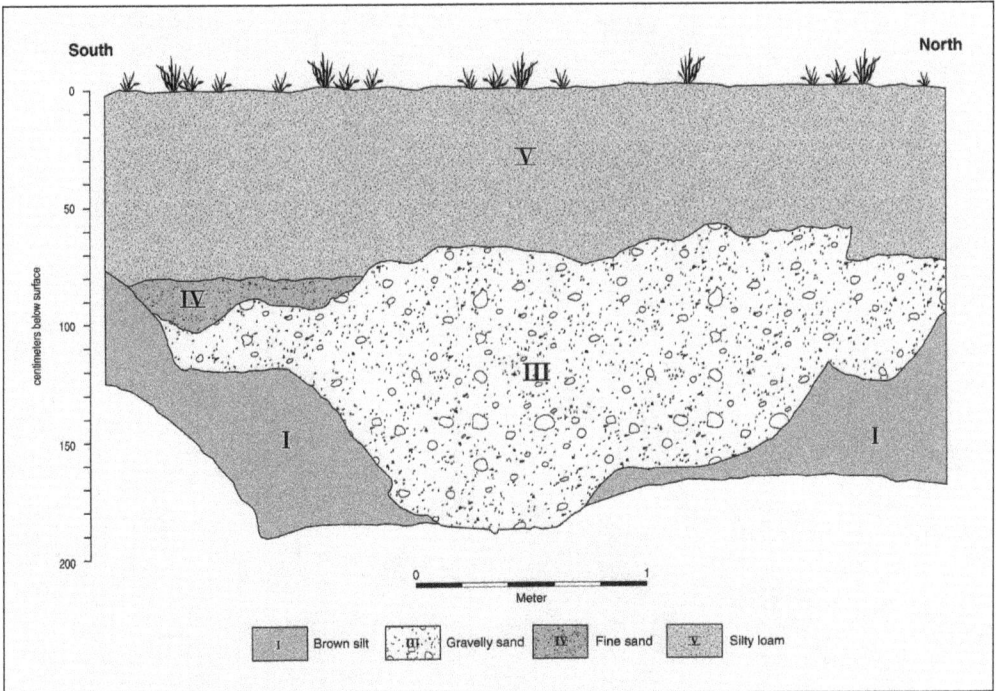

Several excavations have uncovered the exact alignment of the 1819 irrigation ditch, the *zanja*, which is the principal historic resource of the Historic Mission Overlay District. This drawing, from work by Redlands investigator Michael Lerch, shows the form of the *zanja* as it is currently buried along Mission Road. (Courtesy Michael Lerch.)

The Ritchie Mansion, dubbed "Snug Harbor" by its first owner, Capt. Lewis Smith Davis, was substantially rebuilt by Loma Linda University Medical Center and now serves as a guest home for the proton treatment center. (Courtesy Loma Linda University Construction Department.)

Jim and Donna Stocker, Mission Road residents, have supported preservation efforts in many ways, including driving their Model T Ford in the community parade. They are pictured here in front of the historic Frink Adobe.

www.ingramcontent.com/pod-product-compliance
Lightning Source LLC
Chambersburg PA
CBHW050649110426
42813CB00007B/1957